# Thomas Keneally

was born in 1935 and educated in Sydney. His novels
include *The Chant of Jimmy Blacksmith*, *Confederates* and
*Gossip From the Forest* (both shortlisted for the Booker
Prize), as well as *Schindler's Ark*, which won the Booker
Prize in 1982. *The Playmaker*, published in 1987, formed
the basis for an award-winning play, *Our Country's Good*.
He is married and has two daughters.

# THOMAS KENEALLY

# *Now and in Time to Be*

## Ireland and the Irish

Flamingo
*An Imprint of* HarperCollins*Publishers*

Flamingo
An Imprint of HarperCollins*Publishers*,
77–85 Fulham Palace Road,
Hammersmith, London W6 8JB

Published by Flamingo 1992

9 8 7 6 5 4 3 2 1

First published in Great Britain by
Ryan Publishing Co Ltd 1991

Author photograph by Patrick Predergast

The Publisher gratefully acknowledges the following:
Seamus Heaney and Faber & Faber Ltd for excerpts from, 'Ocean's Love
to Ireland', 'Belderg', 'Bog Queen', 'Punishment', 'Strange Fruit', 'The
Grabaulle Man'.
Aidan Carl Mathews and The Gallery Press for an extract from
*Minding Ruth*.
The Estate of James Joyce and Jonathan Cape Ltd for an excerpt from
*A Portrait of the Artist as a Young Man*.
Peter Kavanagh for an extract from *The Complete Poems of Patrick
Kavanagh*.
The Ezra Pound Literary Property Trust and Faber & Faber Ltd for an
extract from *Pavannes and Divagations*.

ISBN 0 00 637 732 7

Set in Galliard

Printed in Great Britain by
HarperCollinsManufacturing Glasgow

For my wife Judith
who supported the intention of this book,
and daughter Margaret
who was an enthusiastic co-traveller
for a slice of this journey,
becoming so enamoured of Ireland
that she now lives in Dublin.

# ACKNOWLEDGEMENTS

These people steered the author in the right direction or saved him from making an utter dingbat of himself in the midst of a complicated nation: Tim Magennis of Bord Fáilte, Professor Gus Martin and his wife Claire, my publisher David Ryan.

The author drew without shame on the great corpus of Irish folksong and verse, and was helped also by a number of books, eminent among them the following:

*Ireland: the Rough Guide* by Doran, Greenwood and Hawkins
*The Troubles* by Ulick O'Connor
*Biting at the Grave and Northern Ireland: Questions of Nuance* by Padraig O'Malley
*Michael Collins* by Tim Pat Coogan
*The Shell Guide to Ireland* by Lord Killanin and Michael V. Duignan
*An Atlas of Irish History* by Ruth Dudley Edwards
*The Fenians in Australia* by Keith Adams
*Ireland: A History* by Robert Kee

These authors, with a host of other Irish commentators, historians, poets and novelists made the grist of this book. To them belongs any small glory and none of the copious blame.

MacDonagh and MacBride
And Connolly and Pearse
Now and in time to be,
Wherever green is worn,
Are changed, changed utterly:
A terrible beauty is born.

from 'Easter 1916' by W.B. YEATS

# The Author's Route

# FOREWORD

On a post-Mass Sunday morning about first pint time, at the south-east Cork port of Ballycotton, I made my lunge at starting this book about Ireland, about the large business of Ireland in itself, and the minuscule question of Ireland and me. I would make second lunges elsewhere, and these would not be wasted, I hoped, but would be sewn into this story somewhere.

One of the starts which didn't take was at Cobh, though I would have put my money on that great harbour so redolent of Irish departures, willed and unwilled. Another was at Newgrange, at the Great Tomb, built by neolithic farmers for the purpose of focussing just one beam of light into a burial chamber at dawn on the year's shortest day. Next lunge was Antrim, at the Giant's Causeway, where I tried to reach for a connection between Fionn MacCumhaill's (pronounced, 'Finn Ma Cool') palaver with a Scottish giant on one hand, and on the other hand the poisonous Orange–Green dialogue up there in Britain's last, most beautiful and saddest province. Fifth, sixth, seventh lunge will all appear in time, and by the time I finish, I may know where to start. Just the same, this account may very well be like the Ireland that's represented in the neolithic tombs in the Boyne: a set of circles carved in stone and lacking an end and a beginning; or instead possessing both at every point.

Even in the spruced-up, economic-rationalist end of the savagely linear twentieth century, Ireland challenges linear explanation and defeats number one lunge, number two, three, and all the others.

THOMAS KENEALLY
Sydney, April 1991

# ONE

I was alone on the cliffs near the fishing village of Ballycotton, Cork. Ballycotton is that kind of fishing port, a *Ryan's Daughter* kind of port, even though it is on the wrong coastline for that, the Cork coastline and not the Dingle Peninsula in Kerry. Ballycotton is a stereotype of the Irish fishing village. Steep streets where Irish families of modest means might spend a week every summer in some tidy guesthouse called the 'Aisling'. A high sea wall raised like a muscular forearm against the ocean, and – though not quite the currachs of Aran – risky-looking fishing boats, rowboats in one or two cases, in others rickety trawlers equipped with radar, nosing out to make free of the sea. An off-harbour island, a peril-to-shipping one with a heavy surf and a lighthouse on its bare, green apex.

Ballycotton fronts a glowering sea, spotlit only here and there by light through the sort of clouds which aren't going to let anyone declare an unambiguous day.

My reason for starting here is that this is the sea my grandparents took to when they – separately – chose to launch themselves on the longest journey of the Irish diaspora – Cork to Australia. These were the cliffs – between here and Cobh – they last saw, and only then if the weather was good. I don't know the answer to any of these questions: did they look back on them from the deck of whatever class they sailed in with a frightful grief, or with a mix of wistfulness and exaltation? Was their young blood really geared up for the longest possible dosage of sea then available to them? Did they think they'd be back to the dear, familiar sights and faces so often invoked in songs of emigration?

> I'm sayin' farewell to the land of my birth
> And the homes that I know so well,
> And the mountains grand of my own native land,
> I'm biddin' them all adieu . . .

On the other hand, were they pleased to see the last of it: the tribalism, the recurrent want, the contumely of being one of Britain's sub-races? Or did they harbour both sets of feelings? In any event, these cliffs were the last they would ever see of Cork or Ireland.

In the North Coast Licensing Court held at Kempsey, New South Wales, Australia, in May 1889, Timothy Thomas Keneally, who has worked well and more or less soberly for a wagon transport company since his arrival in this relatively remote coastal town three hundred miles north of Sydney, applies for the licence of the Pelican Island Hotel. Pelican Island itself is set on a beautiful flood-prone river called the Macleay. Some of the people who drink there are warders from the local Trial Bay prison. This is an experimental gaol, a model prison set on an exquisite beach on the Pacific coast, where prisoners are to be redeemed by building a breakwater. The other customers he hopes for will be dairy farmers and fishermen.

He isn't given the licence outright, he is awarded it provisionally. His affianced, the Licensing Court is told, Kate McKenna of County Clare, is on her way from Cork to Sydney aboard the ship *Woodburn*. When she arrives and marries Timothy, he will be declared licensee in full.

The marriage takes place at Pelican Island in August, 1889,

Kate is only five feet tall, but has a reputation as a no-nonsense, fight-a-tiger-with-a-twig woman. Some might call her a virago. She bears nine children, the youngest my father, eighty-three years old as I write. He would marry a New South Wales country girl, my mother, whose ancestors came from Donegal.

As usual for the grown children of immigrants, he knows little of Kate's motives for travelling such a distance to marry a man she had courted in Ireland. A village scandal, though that seems unlikely? Love? The glory of a pub licence in such a far place? (They called the pub The Harp of Erin, and my father – their youngest child – would always be nicknamed Harper, according to the Australian habit of shortening everything and turning it into a nickname.)

Was she tormented by the last sight of these cliffs across the spotlit sea south of Cobh? Again, her Australian children never asked that question. They seemed to presume that the cooking of their dinner in Pelican Island and, later, in Kempsey, New South Wales, was the one possible destiny on earth open to her.

Now for the first time we encounter a phrase which will recur frequently in this book: *Without being too sentimental* ... Sentiment is the malaise of the returning pilgrim of Irish connection. The sensible native Irish are offended by it. Nonetheless, *without being too sentimental*, I have to say that the loss in some senses must have been a grievous one for her. For what does cause someone from so far away, both in terms of geography and blood descent, to come to Ireland and feel at once a sense of wistful and ecstatic recognition. Is it a matter of grandparental propaganda, murmured in the ear of childhood? Is it things forgotten but absorbed into the fibre?

We people of the diaspora, whether from Australia or Michigan or the plains of Canada, get back here, returning

3

ghosts, utterly confused and in need of guidance; and we see a place like Ballycotton, and recognise it straight away as a never but always known place.

Up on the cliff at Ballycotton then, I notice a girl is reading the *Irish Times* on the doorstep of a house. The name of this cliff house is, according to its gate post, 'Ardanna'. The opposing gate post whimsically translates it thus: 'Annaville'. While the girl reads, another somewhat older woman emerges and speaks to her. She folds the paper and rises from the steps. She has the oval face of which I have heard people say, 'That's a Cork face.' My grandmother possessed it too and gave it to me and my younger daughter Jane. It is sometimes referred to as, 'a potato-face', unjustly, since it can be handsome, especially on the young. The girl follows the woman inside and I can see her through the window joining still another youngish woman and a similarly youngish man. They all sit to tea with their backs to the sea.

The question is, why is this that girl's place, the place where she goes into tea? Why did my grandmother have to travel so far to find the place where her tea was taken?

Kate, variously Kenna, McKenna, lies now in the outer perimeter of Ireland's cure of souls, on a hill in West Kempsey, New South Wales, Australia, looking west to a smoke-blue tangle of hills which she spent all her married life regarding. I have her to thank for my first pair of sandshoes, for my immutably Irish way of saying *theatre* (the-ay-tah) and my dumpling genes. In acquittal of these debts, I decide sentimentally that I should at least be her eyes in Erin of the Harp.

For her sake I had been to Mass in the town of Cloyne. 'Let us pray for the repose of the soul of . . .'

The officiating priest had the same tendency as her to drop aitches not from the front of words but from the back. 'Mont' for month, 'catedral' for cathedral, 'fait' for faith. As an Irish

4

priest should, he seemed to have plenty of homely parables. 'Remember when the new furniture came in, and people couldn't wait to get rid of the old. But then, after a while, people saw the new, mass-produced stuff was shoddy and began to seek the old again. It had enduring value. So it is with the old dogmas we dropped for the sake of the new, flashy, shoddy ones.

'People say, "I'm not a religious person. Could you be saying a prayer for me?" That's' (pronounced grandmother-wise, *dat's*) 'like trying to do a line with a girl and saying to a friend, "Would you be going up to that girl and doing a line for me?"'

Then, at my first Irish Mass, he declared Ireland very worldly. Dangerously secular. Irish clerics the world over always say 'secular' if they want to disapprove of something. Yet, it was hard to believe it of those plain Irish faces in the Cloyne parish church, across from the hurling field with its statue of the great hurler Christy Ring not yet dry from the overnight, autumn storms. Maybe it is true that Ireland's getting worldlier in the strictest theological sense. Yet, in a fundamental sense, it isn't of this world. There is a knowledge legible in those Irish faces in the pews that divine forces will make a mockery of too much cleverness. There is a modesty of hope there, based on the concept that perfection is not meant for the vale of tears. As an American waiting in line for breakfast in Dublin said, 'I suppose if they had all this better organised, they wouldn't be the Irish.' The kingdom is not of this world, and slickness is a tool of the Devil.

That is a philosophic awareness that shapes the life of this island, particularly the Republic's life. But it is there in the average Loyalist Protestant in the North too. The two working classes, who hate each other too much up there, are united in a resistance to the idea that they should become lickety-split model workers, like the Germans or Japanese who are so frequently held up to them as models. Ireland, and Irish history, have made them the one being after all, though they don't know it.

But I get ahead of myself.

# TWO

One wonders then why clerics worry about worldliness while such places as Cloyne exist. Worldliness is hardly the tone in these Irish towns, beneath the towering *memento mori* of the time of Viking terror. How many nations can say that of their provincial towns? That a tenth- or eleventh-century tower is their tallest structure? Towers built in times of Viking raids. Stone spaceships aimed for a safe sky. Anti-Viking towers at sublime Glendalough in Wicklow, at Ardmore in Waterford, at Antrim in Antrim.

The famous ninth-century monk's quatrain:

> Bitter the wind tonight,
> combing the sea's hair white:
> from the North, no need to fear
> the proud sea-coursing warrior.

The doorway is high up in the side, and everyone used to say this was so that the monks could bring all the villagers in, with supplies and weapons, then draw the ladder up and close everyone in. Now there is a scholarly argument that the door was so high for structural reasons. But such questions are picayune compared to what the tower stands for: terror and flight, then a drawing up of whole families into the air, the tower's momentary claustrophobia. And then, a drawn breath, a marital or parental word of reassurance, and the sweet sense of impregnable refuge. The tower is a stratagem of compassion.

7

A people can't live under such towers for a millennium and not have some of that sink in; all aspects of it: the sense of siege, the sense of deliverance, the long, historic prayers funnelled skywards by the monks' stone tubes.

Next after the tower, in supposedly worldly Cloyne as elsewhere, there stand the devastated abbey, and the Norman cathedral. In 1570, the native Gaelic Irish were locked out of this cathedral – named for the monastic leader Colmán mac Lenane, who lived in the seventh century and was an admirable fellow, a professional poet before he became a monk.

In other parts of Ireland, particularly the West, the Catholics hung on to the old religious sites a little longer than 1570. And in some places there was a temporary recapture, as happened with the Cistercian Abbey in Galway, where the Mass was expelled in 1561 and returned eighty-two years later under the pro-Royalist Confederation of Kilkenny. The Augustinians in that city seem to have stayed in place till 1731, probably through influence and being what is now called good corporate citizens. But in Cloyne, as in so many places, the decree was absolute. The Irish were locked out of their church.

Maybe Colmán would have seen a sort of poetic injustice in all this. He was the first Irish poet to write in Latin verse, the first of a wave of song writers who would supply the courts of Europe with their lyrics.

How consistent is his voice with that of later Ireland. Nostalgia for place is dominant:

> So, since your heart is set on those sweet fields
> And you must leave me here,
> Swift be your going, heed not any prayers,
> Although the voice be dear.

A rehearsal – Colmán seemed to be – for all the songs of departure which would bleed down on the ear through Ireland's history.

The Irish like to say that they kept rhyme and the deft phrase alive in the decayed body of the Roman empire, in Dark Ages Europe. And if you read the ninth-century *Triads*, translated by Thomas Kinsella, you see how well the civilised concerns of those times, bright in Ireland, dimmer elsewhere, lasted into twentieth-century Ireland:

> Three excellent qualities in narration: a good flow, depth of
> thought, conciseness.
> Three dislikeable qualities in the same: stiffness, obscurity, bad
> delivery.
> Three things that are always ready in a decent man's house:
> beer, a bath, a good fire.
> Three accomplishments well regarded in Ireland: a clever verse,
> music on the harp, the art of shaving faces . . .

When the Christian Brothers in Sydney told me that Ireland was the Land of Saints and Scholars, I looked at them and wondered what they meant in a world of muscular priests, policemen, publicans, railway workers and footballers who were the only people with Irish names I knew and whose saintliness and scholarship didn't strike me as their prime characteristics. But the Brothers were speaking of men like Colmán, of course. They meant the wave he started, the native Irish tradition of letters which was mediated down to me, in humid classrooms in Homebush, New South Wales, Australia, in that single term: Land of Saints and Scholars.

Cloyne has the visible symbols of Irishdom: the unworldliness, the Norse tower, the cathedral closed to the Mass in 1571, the plain nineteenth-century native church, built opposite the hurling field. For nearly four hundred years, the Catholics had to keep their *stations*, their meetings for Mass and other devotional purposes, in homes and fields and by the poignant Mass-stones you sometimes see beside country roads. All this is part of the race memory the nineteenth-century peasant Irish

9

have passed on to their descendants, even to those in the New World. All this has gone to feed the politics and the follies of Ireland. For only the Slavs have a race memory to match that of the Irish.

The priest at Cloyne that Sunday announced *stations* which would be held in various homes in the locality throughout the rest of winter. The devotional practices of persecution lasting in the Irish Republic. As if there was a cohesion and warmth in those old clandestine meetings which may be lacking in the plain churches of the post-Emancipation. *Stations* were often very popular amongst the Irish in the Australian bush, where families could be separated from the nearest church by a hundred and fifty miles or more. Again, Australia is a long way for the habits of Penal Days to travel.

*

It is a matter for sadness that the Catholic churches of Ireland lack the authority of the old Norman and Romanesque places from which politics locked the native Irish out of in the sixteenth century, or which Elizabethan or Cromwellian troops fired. The nineteenth century was a poor time for architectural taste, and so the church building which went on throughout Ireland produced few temples of distinction. The Catholic cathedral in Waterford is an exception, and a symbol of the contradictions of Irish society: the site was granted by the city corporation, which was Protestant, in Penal Times, the early 1790s. It has a French look, and was probably influenced by Saint-Sulpice and other places in Paris where Irish clergy had studied. The great St Colmán's cathedral in Cobh, high above the port, built in the 1830s as if to ensure that the last steeple the departing Irish would see, is – as they say – good of its kind, designed by Pugin, the star of that Gothic Revival a lot of people wish hadn't happened.

But the general level of post-Penal clerical architecture is better represented by the hideous cathedral in Galway, which the locals call the Taj Michael after the Galway bishop Michael (Mee-hall) Brown.

Fault for flat nineteenth- and twentieth-century churches lay not only with the Catholic clergy. The clergy of the Church of Ireland, who had inherited such wonderful buildings, spent money and energy vulgarising their interiors. Lord Killanin writes scathingly of a nineteenth-century 'restoration' of the nave of St Colmán's in Cloyne.

Again, Protestant landlords and Church of Ireland bishops were often very generous in helping set up Catholic churches which the serfs and tradespeople attended. In my grandfather's village of Newmarket, Cork, for example, the landlords of the fine Georgian house, which still stands on the hill on the south side of the village, were the Aldsworth family. The Aldsworths donated the altar of the Newmarket Catholic church – it is based on the design of a sixth-century altar from Iona, the monastic settlement of Columba or Columbkille, another of those Saints and Scholars of the 500s and so on whom I heard about in the pre-lunch Christian doctrine segment of my education in Homebush, New South Wales, Australia.

Similarly, in the straight-up-and-down post-Penal Catholic church in Cloyne there's a tribute to the Church of Ireland Bishop of Cloyne who helped greatly with the building expenses of this church. One wonders what blend of decency, compassion, expedient desire to get on with the natives, who were so often the labourers and servants, contributed to this philanthropy. How fascinating it must have been to observe, as Edith Somerville and Violet Ross did in *Some Memoirs of an Irish R.M.*, how all the elements of an Irish community in the nineteenth century were kept for so many years in comity and balance. It is really not the rebellions of Ireland which should astound us. It is the long phases of *modus vivendi*.

\*

In Cloyne as in any Irish town on a Sunday, a visit to a post-Mass pub brings you up against the anti-clericalism of the Irish. Yet in a way, even the priest-hatred of Ireland is a tribute to the power of the Church. In *The Field*, John B. Keane's tragic play, Bull McCabe's anti-clericalism won't take him *in past* the doorway of the church, but the power of the clergy won't let him actually stay away. Half-observant, half-rebellious, he scuffs his boots at the steps of the temple.

You always hear those heady anti-clerical moans in Sunday pubs from Malin Head to Waterford. You might conclude, if you didn't know the Irish better, that the days of the clergy were numbered. It happened that in the pub in Cloyne that morning, men – who keep the flame of anti-clericalism safe here, away from their wives – were talking about how the Irish hierarchy had most lately gone to trouble to make themselves look silly. These men, who were capable of compassion when addressing some social issues and when speaking of distant evils like the relationship between famine and politics in the Third World, had brought down what looked like a mean-minded statement on Irish weddings. Couples should not have the right to choose the music for their wedding ceremonies. Not only were secular love songs right out, but so were theologically inappropriate old standards like Ave Maria. Just because it was your wedding day, you couldn't let the soprano loose in the choir loft, and long-haired friends of the couple who happened to have a guitar and a repertoire of Dylan ballads would not be admitted.

On the radio, the captain of the Cork hurling team and his beloved, who were getting married that weekend, sounded both disgruntled and philosophic about it all. 'But I'm a Catholic,' the girl said, 'and if you're a Catholic you have to do it their way.'

What a wealth of meaning lies in that phrase, '*their way*'.

12

The Irish are as paradoxical about the Church as about all politics. Sometimes they choose to see it as their own possession, a fountain of spiritual comfort for the dispossessed; and at other times as something like a bank or insurance company where the Board – the hierarchy – sets the interest rates.

A bishop who had defended the decision on radio indicated that there was no intrusion on the rights of the couple. They simply chose the music in consultation with the priest. A man in a cap. Ireland's representative man, away from the social controls of the women, and speaking for wry, one-pint-down, two-to-go men all over Ireland, for men who would have their dark say and then go home to the Blessed Virgin at the hearth and the Sacred Heart above the marriage bed – this man said, 'Isn't that like deciding how much tax you're going to pay in friendly consultation with the tax man.'

Since the returning visitor to Ireland always thinks partly according to the iconography of rebellion, just as a visitor to New Mexico thinks of Apaches, I thought in Cloyne, during all this disapproval of bishops and their hegemony over music, of a certain Father Herrold (sometimes spelled Harold in the records) of Wicklow, transported to Australia after the 1798 rebellion aboard a convict transport out of Cobh named *Minerva*. Because they feared that through his sacramental powers he served as a centre of sedition in New South Wales, the British administrators made him watch every flogging of an Irish prisoner, hoping he would be thereby chastened. His dignity through all these demonstrations of savagery, and the subtle succour he gave the victims, further disgruntled the authorities, who were not large-minded men, who were the sort of second-stringers you'd expect to find at the earth's end, running such a sideshow. As soon as it could be arranged, they shipped him home again on condition that his bishop, who had never in any case approved of his activities, would stand surety for him and supervise him.

I cannot imagine that, after seeing the flesh and gristle fly in barbarous New South Wales, Father Herrold would have been too fussed about the theological exactness of wedding tunes.

But you can't tell. The compassion and the fixity often exist in the same man. So, maybe I was being too sentimental about brave Father Herrold. In any case, in his liberation theology, in his passive rebelliousness, he was a fair model of the Irish priesthood at its most robust and loving.

\*

I knew in Cloyne that I would ultimately make it all the way round Ireland – if the roads and the weather permitted – to Maynooth, the great Catholic seminary created by the British to ensure that the clergy would produce no further priests like Father Herrold or brave Father Murphy, a leader of the 1798 rebellion celebrated in the folksong 'Boolavogue'. A seminary I had studied in as a child had been based on the Maynooth model, as most of the seminaries in the English-speaking world would be.

Yet as we will see, even in the licit spruced-up priesthood of the nineteenth and early twentieth century, even from Maynooth, the rebels as well as the straight-down-the-line men came. And again, it was often the case that the two characteristics were incorporated in the one man. We see that in the case of Archbishop Mannix of Melbourne, who was considered such a dangerous nationalist after he had led a successful campaign to prevent the conscription of Australians for the Western Front, that the British sent a Royal Naval vessel to intercept his steamer and prevent him landing in Ireland. And in the case of Archbishop Clune, who tried to carry to Lloyd George accurate and balanced information about the state of Ireland and the depredations of British security forces. Both were brave, good men, but both were capable of narrow and doctrinaire stances.

14

The doggedness of some of the clergy and laity has a connection with the image of Ireland which the Irish of the diaspora try to push. That is based on the virtues of full-bloodedness, pugnacity, forthrightness and egalitarianism, whimsy and song. It ignores the other, though just as obvious, aspects of the national character: the tight-lipped and claustrophobic respectability of both clergy and laity, and the eight-hundred-years-practised appeasing reverence for one's betters. The laughers of Ireland, you find quickly enough once you're actually there, are balanced out by the dour and the canonical.

You might be able to believe otherwise in McGovern's Bar in Reade Street in Manhattan, at Eamonn Doran's up on Second Avenue at 52nd, in Michael Durkins's pub in the Rocks in Sydney, with an antipodean Irish band called the Irish Drovers belting out 'Viva La Quinta Brigada'. But the myth doesn't survive a Sunday spent in any Irish town.

Cloyne is a good instance.

# THREE

So the first cliffs are Ballycotton, and the first Mass is Cloyne and the first house is Ballymaloe. At other times in Ireland I've stayed in farmhouses: for example, when my daughters were little and seeing the place for their first time, wondering perhaps why I made such a fuss of it when Australia was so much sunnier. In the farmhouses you got a lot for a little: local anecdotes and prejudices stated forthrightly – but so as not to offend – over the dinner table; a large soft bed, again under the welcome patronage of the Sacred Heart or the Virgin. Sometimes the farmhouse would be a flash, new one, brick and wide windows. It might be called by a Gaelic name, or even in some cases by the surname of a pope – I noticed that Roncalli was popular.

I remember sitting up late one night with a farmer, after the girls were abed, drinking hot whiskeys spiked with cloves and sweetened with honey, and being treated to the sort of flamboyant lateral thinking, the kind of utterance the Irish are given to and which you don't know whether they utter to impress the stranger, or because it's their nature to think this way, or both.

In any case, holding his honeyed tincture to the firelight, this man said, 'I've been taking this three months now for my cold.' (We were then located in Clare, where Katy Kenna came from, and like Katy and the priest of Cloyne, the farmer was bereft of 'th', as Australians are bereft of 'a's.) 'Tree monts for me cold. And praise be to God, it hasn't done it the least bit of good.'

Many of the farmhouses we stayed at were run by some of that one-tenth of the population of the Republic which is not Catholic. I remember there was a beautiful one in Ballydavid, over near the Blaskets, on the Dingle Peninsula. It was run by a youngish widow with three or four children. Indisputably Irish – for, after all, her ancestors had been there hundreds of years longer than ninety-nine per cent of American families have been in America, and Ireland was beloved to her as it was to anyone.

Later, when I went to Utah, I saw an echo of her condition. She was definitely a Utahn. But she was a Gentile amongst the Mormons; for in Utah they call all non-Mormons, even the Jews, Gentiles. Gentiles are citizens, but they have a sense that they may at any stage fail subtle – or even overt – tests. Mind you, the comparison with Utah is a harsh one, and is intended as a figure of speech rather than a scientifically exact statement. In the Republic, the Irish Catholics do not have commerce tied up, the way the Mormons do in Utah. And the Irish go more for the crooked, ironic grin rather than the orthodontic smile of terrifying goodwill you encounter in Salt Lake.

Another farmhouse we visited at that time was in County Laois. We were delayed some days by the generosity of the farmer and his wife, elderly folk whose ancestors had come to Ireland to serve in Henry Ireton's Parliamentary Army in 1651. For their campaigning against the Irish, they had been given this modest parcel of land. At the stage their successors hit us with their huge country breakfasts, the family had been farming this land for three and a quarter centuries. Indistinguishable from the Irish rural bulk except in his separate, Protestant heritage, the farmer had a good eye for blackthorn branches ('blacktorn' he called it, again just like Kate Kenna). He

17

could fashion them into finished walking sticks with a few swipes of his knife.

He told me once about something I'd never thought of while I was receiving an education in Mass-stones and hedge schools from the Christian Brothers in Sydney: how tough it was for a rural Protestant lad like him to find a girlfriend and then a bride when he was young. You couldn't bowl up to the local dance and ask anyone at all to do the two-step with you. Descendants of Ireton's hard-nosed Cromwellian other-ranks did not go off to Dublin or England to school and university. They did not subsist in a populous upper class of their own. They were limited, when it came to everything from dancing and flirtation to taking a partner for life, to such a small minority. He told me this briefly, without labouring it. It had all the more force for that. It was just another case of the way history, wearing the face of religious observance, keeps people skewered in Ireland.

This journey, the journey of this book, I wasn't going to the farmhouses and the bed-and-breakfasts, though I frequently passed them and sometimes called in for tea. This time I was staying in houses of the kind to whose front door Katy Kenna would have been unlikely to be admitted. Houses built in the eighteenth or nineteenth century by the Anglo-Irish gentry. They often stand on or near the ruins of earlier versions: which belonged to Irish Confederates and were fired by Cromwell's troops; which belonged to Plantation landlords and were fired by Irish Confederates; which were burned by James's or William's forces in the late 1680s, or by British militias or by rebels in 1798, or by Black and Tans or Republicans in the early 1920s.

These surviving fine houses, so often built on the ruins of earlier ones, are now too expensive to maintain as anything but hotels.

My first house was Ballymaloe House near Cloyne, run by

a couple called the Allens whose cooking is famous. Is there any such thing as Irish cooking? asks the gourmand snootily. The question would not survive an evening before Ivan and Myrtle's enormous table.

Though I am travelling part of the way alone – though it will be Donegal before my now grown daughter joins me for a while – I see for the first time that I am going to be a fortunately billeted man. Though it has never been burned, Ballymaloe partakes of that sort of representative history I mentioned above. In 1578–83, during the Munster wars in which the poet Edmund Spenser served on the English side, Ballymaloe's corn and cattle were plundered by the Elizabethan forces. In 1602, the owner John Fitzgerald was knighted here by Lord Mountjoy for staying neutral during the Battle of Kinsale, of which something will be said later. But in the early seventeenth century, Lady Honoria Fitzgerald hid monks here, along with a relic which is now in the Dominican priory in Cork. In 1641, the house passed to Lord Broghill, who would become a Cromwellian. Cromwell would stay here, and so would William Penn, Admiralty Clerk in Kinsale and later Pennsylvania's father. Then the house passed to a succession of Anglo-Irish owners, who gradually rebuilt it in its present charming form. The Lichfield family owned it for over a hundred years until 1948, when Ivan Allen took it over and eventually opened its dining room, The Yeats Room.

The house is full of eighteenth- and nineteenth-century paintings which belong there historically – there's fascination in that too. They hung on the walls at the time the owners used to send their daughters up to the season at Dublin Castle and to the summer liveliness of the watering hole called Mallow in North Cork. Apart from the extraordinary seafood, veals, hams and poultries, what everyone remembers of the house is the painting of an eighteenth-century midget and servant called Chuff, who served here under his master John Corker in the early 1700s. Chuff's portrait, along with that of the Georgian horse Jester, were missing from the house from the mid-1830s until the Allens tracked them down and restored them in the late 1960s, the period when Ballymaloe opened its doors to guests.

*

The only problem with these houses was that they were not always lively with conversation. People came here from Europe and America and Dublin for a quiet time, so that an Australian writer alone had to exercise some conversational deftness to get friendships going. But I did not resent that too much. I do not intend to pursue the mawkish idea that I really represent my five-foot granny in these places. But I did have some leisurely sense of letting my grandmother's blood find its ease in these fine rooms, and before the superb Irish produce of the field and the sea. At Ivan and Myrtle's table in the evenings, I liked to indulge a dangerous illusion for the portly: the concept that I was eating for two.

By day I would travel far from Ballymaloe, taking notes and working energetically. I wasn't sure whether it might develop into the sort of book where I would need to know about the round tower and the beautiful Romanesque figure carvings in the gable of the wrecked twelfth-century cathedral at Ardmore, a sea port as stereotypically beautiful as Ballycotton, but lifted out of the ordinary by that stone frieze of the Fall, the Judgement of Solomon and the Adoration of the Magi. I wasn't sure whether I needed to know if the cathedral is based on the monastic site of another Irish hero, St Declan, whose holy well is on the cliff at Ardmore.

I thought you might need to know too about the remarkable fort called Charles at the entrance to Kinsale, perhaps the most beautiful port in an island of exquisite ones. I thought you might need to know how long lovely Kinsale was occupied by the Spaniards (1601–2), or how Hugh O'Neill of Ulster's brave nine-year struggle against the Tudors, the fight from which Sir John Fitzgerald of Ballymaloe abstained, came to an end here when he tried to link up with the Spaniards and was defeated.

I thought likewise you would need to know about Youghal, a market town and fishing port on the Blackwater Estuary. I thought you might require me to remark that it was probably Saxon in origin, definitely Anglo-Norman in occupation from the thirteenth century onwards. Part of Sir Walter Ralegh's vast land grant where, so the apocryphal story goes, he first planted the potato on Irish soil! All the more potency to Seamus Heaney's brilliant poem on the subject of Ralegh and Ireland, and what a doomed attraction that was, and how the potato he first planted, even though he didn't do it in Youghal, bound the native Irish to a bitter hunger in the future:

> Speaking broad Devonshire,
> Ralegh has backed the maid to a tree
> As Ireland is backed to England . . .

I thought you might need to know the date of the Youghal Clock Gate, too. It's hard to know at the start what is expected. I had an ambition to produce an Ireland of my own which would be of interest to readers, but I wasn't sure I could go halfway towards doing it simply on the basis of my grandmother's credit as a ghost in this landscape, without myself knowing about the clock tower.

But it was not always the question of whether a given port had a Viking origin or a Norman one that galvanised the traveller. It was, for example, the wild places – the Munster Way and the Knockmealdown Mountains, between say Clonmel and Lismore, the places which stink of an irreducible Irish paganism and of the penance of the Anchorites of that first wave of monasticism, when men came from Brittany or Wales

21

or Italy (they say St Patrick could have come from any of those three) to occupy stone cells in places where the earth and its gods, and all the ambiguous spirits of the night which have haunted the Irish imagination, are so predominant.

And it was not only the wild places. It was the accidental salient detail which, in travel as in the novel, meant the most. It was for instance finding a graveyard, fairly ill-kempt, in the Drum Hills above Dungarvan, where famine victims were buried. The local community had spruced up the site and placed a memorial on the mute turf to mark a papal visit ten years back. Peasants on the road. Starving peasants always take to the road, in Ethiopia at the barbarous end of this century, in Ireland in the barbarous middle of the last. I stood on a hill like that and knew from what I had seen of the skeletal Ethiopians and Eritreans how the starved Irish looked on the edge of death. How hunger had impelled them along roads but now nailed them to this hill. Were they coming from the direction of Cork, or were they climbing out of Waterford Country? Since this is not a regular churchyard, it means someone merciful brought all those who had died on the ascent to this point to this spot for burial.

That hunger which was the beginning of Ireland's population decline. That hunger so emblematic in the politics of every place the Irish went – New York, Melbourne, Otago in New Zealand. That terrible sign occurs all over Ireland – Famine Graves. It always leads to a paddock bearing either no mark at all or a small stone monument. The chief markers are not in the geography but all in the brain.

From the ghosts of the Famine to Ballymaloe's feast! Fortunate in my time, and lucky so far . . .

# FOUR

My Irish-descended relatives in the bush would, in my child-hood, never begin a journey without three Hail Marys for a safe arrival. I know why that was now. It was the memory of Irish roads.

It is a matter of credit that this is a country lacking in freeways, except for rare stretches like the one near Limerick which sweeps the tourist from Shannon Airport to Bunratty Castle. Bunratty's Disney-esque reputation is such that people believe it was built especially for tourism. The castle is a real castle, built by the MacNamaras in the 1460s. During the Irish uprising of 1641, the one which would bring the Curse of Cromwell down on Ireland, it served as a refuge for planted English and Scots. Now it has been restored. It puts on medieval feasts and has a Folk Park where tweeds and sweaters and jaunty hats can be bought. And a freeway runs there from Shannon Airport.

But it doesn't last any further. Even the main highways, Limerick to Killarney, Killarney to Cork, Cork to Waterford, Waterford to Dublin, Dublin to Newry, Newry to Coleraine, Coleraine to Derry – even these are real roads, roads you know you're travelling on. Given that normal mix of stubborn conservatism and debonair recklessness with which various of the Irish drive, even for these main arteries you need three Hail Marys or any other ritual you feel you can depend on.

Motorists wave to each other in Ireland. This doesn't happen anywhere else except in remotest Australia and in cattle towns in Wyoming. I am sure that no collision occurs in Ireland without a fraternal or sisterly wave preceding it.

The realest roads, the most beautiful and the most perilous, are the country ones. Examples of them: there's a high, narrow, awestruck road over the Caha Mountains from Glengariff to Kenmare. Bantry Bay, that is, to Kenmare River. On the right day it will keep you honest. At random: another runs from Ballybofey via Glenties and Ardara down to Glencolumbkille (or Gleann Cholm Cille). Here's another one for those who like to arrive with a sense not of routine but of deliverance: Recess (Sraith Salac) to Kylemore to Letterfrack to Cleggan. The R476 from Ennis to Corrofin in Clare encouraged me to yearn for the lost certainties of the rosary; a quaking decade would have been a great soother. As it was I had to fall back on humanist assurances that the statistics for brain damage in accidents on such lanes are probably lower than you would expect. I won't bore you with other lists of superb but perilous thoroughfares from Monaghan, Mayo, Sligo, Donegal, Cavan, Meath, Wicklow and so on.

These country roads are roads which you know have been built for pilgrims and cattle. Here, as nowhere else in Europe, you are made to travel at a reflective pace. The men who drive the herds down these narrow ways look as though livestock are very important to them. You don't dare nudge the flanks or shoulders of any beast. Local people often drive through herds with a blackthorn in their window-side hands, uttering thick curses and pushing and thwacking flanks. It's still not fast work to get through. One day over near the cliffs of Moher, I drove in a gale in the midst of an ambling herd for half an hour.

Sometimes the roads are for games too. There have been till modern times few suppositions that traffic is more important than games. Once in Cork, my progress to Clonakilty was held up by a jovial man who raised his hand and came to the window to ask me would I mind waiting. His hands were full of the enormous Irish banknotes which have since been replaced by smaller, niftier coins. There was, he said, a 'bahling contest' on between two local champions. 'Fellas have a lot of money on this one if you don't mind, sir.'

Two contestants sling a ball along a country road for a given number of miles. If the road doubles back on itself, they are allowed to throw cross-country, but there are penalties if they land in the rough. This must be an ancient game, maybe a Celtic version of the principle exploited by American Indians in the game which ultimately became known as lacrosse.

If you want to be strict-minded about it, you could say such a plain thing as that Irish roads reflect Ireland's small tax base. But they also, of course, reflect something of the Irish spirit. The compulsory wave reminds me of the impulse Australian males have to call everyone 'mate' as a means of showing they don't think they're better than anyone. So the Irish driver says, 'Just because I'm on the wrong side of the road doesn't mean at all that I'm denying your right to be here.'

Irish roads are therefore where citizens of flashier and more arrogant nations go to be reduced to an appropriately human scale of progress. Not only by means of the highways' narrowness and peril; nor by means of their frequent black spots – a black circle on white – which mark the places where someone has gone too suddenly to his death. But also by means of their packed detail and their recurring beauty.

\*

In the Burren, say, a weird stretch of limestone in the north of Clare, you will travel on a span of road which seems too narrow to permit two vehicles to pass at the same time. You will nudge your vehicle up against a stone wall to let the occasional petrol tanker driven by a waving Irishman to pass. But you will be a peril to others too, since the landscape is so crammed with continual weird wonders and human remnants. The pumice landscape, for a start. *The Rough Guide* quotes Cromwell's lieutenant-general in West Clare, Edmund Ludlow: 'Savage land, yielding neither water enough to drown a man, nor a tree to hang him, nor soil enough to bury him.' Precisely the sort of report which left the region a Gaelic outpost for so long. It is the sort of country too which has made the Irish and the traveller revert either to the inner sweetness of Christ – in the case of sixth-century Anchorites and others; or to the more palpable consolations: the turf fire, the bowl of punch, and a warm woman – probably, in the Burren, named O'Loughlin – on your knee. It seems barely to have succumbed to occupation, and the road edges its way like a servant, careful not to bump up against the bony realities of the place.

\*

At a road junction here stands the ruin of Leamaneh Castle, which brings its broad vacant windows and demesne wall right up to the road junction, a Gaelic dream home, ambitious in its architecture, four storeys high, splendid in its floorless, roofless condition, and in this desolation a sermon on human vanity. Built throughout the embattled 1640s by Conor O'Brien and his wife Mary Ni Mahon, the fabled Maire Rua whose name is invoked throughout the Burren; finished in the very year the Catholic Confederacy collapsed; said to have been burned by Cromwell's troops. (In this case they were innocent, though they occupied it for twenty years.)

Once you saw the house, you would then want to cross the field behind the ruin to Cathair Scribin, the ringfort you clearly see from the road. Ah, those drystone ringforts. So deftly made before Christ by the newly arrived Celts. Inside, a rampart and walkway. Beautiful work. As affecting in its way as the workmanship of Leamaneh itself. Some of them have souterrains, underground passages beginning under the walls and used either for shelter from missiles or for food storage.

If you take the road west from Maire Rua's Leamaneh, you pass within a short walk of a dozen of these energetically raised forts, so that you get the impression the Burren must have been a turbulent region in the Celtic era, with lots of raiding and cattle stealing in progress under the aegis of that deity of cattle-theft, Cúchulainn. There are occasional barrow graves too, before you reach the town of Kilfenora. It rewards you with its five standing Celtic crosses amongst and around the ruins of the old cathedral. One of them is post-Reformation, but the others mark Kilfenora's monastic and ecclesiastical beginnings.

If instead of going to Kilfenora, you take the road north from Maire Rua's ruined great house you pass, as you go north, further cathairs, but also standing stones and what are called portal or doorway dolmens, erected for religious and burial purposes by pre-Celtic people. Some of the features are impossible to pass by. The ruins of a medieval village stand right opposite a lonely but neat EC-style farmhouse. The name of the place is Carron, and its unroofed church stands on a small escarpment. Nearby is a holy well, Tobar Chaimin, which is believed to cure sore eyes. A little north, at Poulnabrane, stands a really fine portal dolmen – a large flat rock lifted onto standing-rock supports. It is fifteen yards from the road. There is nowhere to park, but you'll park anyhow. That's why travel is slow in Ireland.

Peter Haden, the owner of Gregan's Castle, a fine house whose dining room looks out over the Burren's wiry landscape, directed me to a particular ringfort, a really superb one which would have commanded the glen which culminated at the town of Ballyvaughan. It was a sort of headquarters fort, and the Burren lords, the O'Loughlins, would build their medieval stronghold just below it.

If I could draw away from the Burren for a moment, I must say I became quite taken with ringforts, with three in particular on the mainland (Dun Aengus, a really sinister one, is on Aran, so I'll mention it later).

First, this one Peter Haden directed me to; then the beautiful Staigue fort in Kerry, high up towards the head of a glen and looking down over an enormous lowland on the broad mouth of the Kenmare River. And finally, the superb, restored Grianan of Aileach, built in the Iron Age but maintained by the O'Neills because it commands so superbly the whole estuary of the Foyle above Derry.

Is any country more crammed with failed fortifications than Ireland?

*

John Betjeman said the Burren people are 'Europe's last Stone Age people', a reference to the belief that you hear uttered in places like Ballyvaughan that the three main clans of the Burren date from the New Stone Age, that the Burren has been a closed genetic system up into modern times. Like Lieutenant-General Ludlow, few outsiders wanted much to do with the Burren. Throughout the Church of Ireland, it was the least popular diocese. Cromwell's soldiers no doubt moaned about their posting here, to Leamaneh, and they must have made some genetic input, despite the intractability of the natives. Nonetheless, you don't have to look far around Ballyvaughan or Kilfenora to find the sort of extraordinary faces which match Betjeman's claim. But then, Ireland is good at casting up the striking face required to prove any theory of history or genetics.

The area I am describing – Kilfenora to Ballyvaughan by way of the wreckage of Maire Rua's home – is possibly ten or twelve miles. The distance between trees in some parts of Australia. Such is the intensity of Irish travel.

\*

On a penitentially narrow, stone-fringed road in Galway I gave a lift to a small, red-haired woman with a backpack. There are few countries in Western Europe where hitchhiking can be so safely done, at little peril for both the driver and the passenger.

It turned out that this woman was a poet. Her first book of verse was about to be published by Raven Arts Press in Dublin. I was very pleased to be in Yeats's country with his potential successor.

She was intelligent and knew a great deal of the world. So I was very careful not to present her with the normal soulfulness of the dispersed Irish back for a visit; the dogged condolence which is typical of those who have become something else yet believe they are still of Ireland's whole cloth.

I was tentative and apologetic about talking of the melancholy of Ireland. To me though it's so inescapable. The vacancies and the ghosts. You wouldn't even have to know anything about the history to see it, but the history helps. Yet I noticed that the Irish were impatient with you for referring to the melancholy. They were getting to a stage of their history where they wanted to be positive. And besides, it was their sadness, and they'd fitted it into their scheme of life, and they didn't want you coming along and overbalancing everything with the weight of your glib emotion.

I realised that the wistfulness of the returner – as I apologised to the woman – must drive the natives crazy. Here they are, attempting to fit in as good citizens of the European Community and signatories of the European Unity Act and fans of U2. But the roads are crammed with effusive foreigners, their brains a pastiche of bits of ballad, of folk and family memory, all of them determined not to associate Ireland with the future, but to rivet it to its past, while at the same time complaining about the narrowness of the roads!

I had noticed the same phenomenon in Israel: honest and practical Israelis are often impatient with fervid New Jersey Jews, or Palestinians with the city intellectuals of Amman or Damascus. For it is true that nothing is owned more intimately by a people than their tragedies, that no outsider should, on whatever grounds, try to horn in.

The poet listened tolerantly to me as I spoke, but she was on to more exciting stuff. She told me about a country house, now an An Óige (Youth) Hostel in Doorus near Kinvara, where she'd stayed the night before. The hostel had once been the country house of the preposterously named Count Floribund de Basterot, who entertained there not only Guy de Maupassant and Paul Bourget, but also the leading figures of the Irish Revival – Yeats, Lady Gregory, A.E. (George Russell), and Douglas Hyde, the founder of the Gaelic League. There one afternoon in 1897, when Yeats and Lady Gregory were stuck indoors escaping the rain, they began to discuss the establishment of a theatre likely to perform their work, especially work derived from the Irish folklore of the West. The theatre they pledged themselves to that afternoon was eventually established just after Christmas 1904. It was the Abbey, Ireland's massive gift to the world of drama.

It wasn't quite accurate, perhaps, to say that a fortuitous shower at Doorus generated the Abbey, but it was nearly so.

And so she accentuated the positive, and the visitor from sun-struck Australia wept over the steering wheel, keeping time with the driving rain beyond the windscreen and telling all the sad Celtic tales to a Celt.

She may not have been a Celt anyway, of course, despite her red hair. Because her home town was Ennis originally, and if her ancestors had spent centuries in Ennis, then it must be recognised that it was a great centre of settlement by the

Normans and the English. But I think we'd have to say that this talented young woman was at least a demi-Celt.

So I confessed to her that I didn't know if it was childhood conditioning – whether it was what the St Joseph nuns told me in the room in Wauchope, New South Wales, where on Sunday the priest put his vestments on and which the rest of the week was a schoolroom. Or whether it was sudden fumes of anger from grandparents. In any case, I'd never been able to come to Ireland without feeling that it was haunted by absences. Every little stone enclosure, and every cottage whose roof tree had been broken, spoke to me of evictions and forced emigration. After all, I reasoned with this poet, Ireland is the only EC country whose population has declined since 1841, and not just declined, but been reduced by a factor of two or three.

Look at the map in *An Atlas of Irish History* by Ruth Dudley Edwards, the map which shows percentage decline of all Irish counties between 1841 and 1851. It's like looking at a map of, say, White Russia, at the percentages of Jewish population before and after the Holocaust; or it's like confronting the demographics of some African famine. In those ten years, while gold was discovered in America and Australia, while the New World boomed, the population decline in Cork and Clare was twenty-six percent, in Mayo and Sligo twenty-nine percent, and in Roscommon thirty-one percent. Many of these declines were the direct result of the famine, and the rest were from emigration. The numbers signified that Ireland by 1851 must have been in a stunned condition akin to that of Europe as a whole at the end of the Black Death. It is my suspicion, I told her, though I couldn't argue it, that Ireland has *never* recovered, that the trauma remains and is habitual, that as with a paralysis the Irish have got used to it only because it has been the established pattern.

And the figures seem palpable to me in the Irish land-scape. Those fenced little stony portions in Connemara or in

Derryveagh stand for those figures, either the figures of that terrible decade or the equally and persistently alarming figures for subsequent decades.

I told the poet about a woman I was giving a lift to in County Galway who said almost idly, 'My cousin left for Australia from that very house there.' She pointed to a farmhouse of the older style, the kind which even twenty years ago would have been thatched but which has since received a slate roof. It was the habitual way she said it, as if, of course, that was what cousins did. It seems astonishing to me, I told the poet, that the Irish have been able to maintain their pride, their identity, their sense of a nation, their application to its present and future, in the face of such endless erosion.

So this was the first sadness I enumerated to the redhead demi-Celt poet.

\*

The second sadness was specific but related to the first. My grandfather was a native of Newmarket in that northern section of Cork called Duhallow. I shall expatiate on Newmarket, probably to the tedium of the reader, in the near future. But the point I made to the poet was that he had six brothers and sisters, and every one of them emigrated either to the United States or to Australia.

Recently, I told her, I'd gone hunting for my great-grandparents' graves in the part of Newmarket known as West End, in a graveyard called Clonfert. There was an autumn gale raging, quite blinding weather, and mud in Duhallow is prime mud indeed. I tried to find the graves of Jeremiah Keneally and Anne MacSwiney amongst the mud and the rain. There were crowds of others of the family name, all at rest there. I was able to find the 1844 grave of my great-great-grandfather Daniel. It struck me as I searched, until the mud and the gale wore out my filial duty, that the miserable part for Jeremiah and

Anne was that none of their emigrant children were at home to follow their bodies up New Street, Newmarket to Clonfert. Every one of the seven was in Australia or America.

I could understand the demi-Celt justifiably thinking, 'So what?' Such tales as mine, which I had harboured sombrely in sun-drenched New South Wales, were Irish commonplaces.

But I had a third sad tale to relate as well. A bottled-in-bond Irish tragic story. This one concerned my wife's great-grandfather: Hugh Larkin or Lorcan, a convict born at Laurencetown, County Galway. Laurencetown is in fertile eastern Galway, south of Ballinasloe. Hugh Larkin was sentenced at Galway on 29 July 1833 to transportation for life for the offence called: 'Assaulting Habitation'. In a letter of petition to Dublin Castle, his wife Esther would say that he had been sentenced for 'Terry-Altism'; the Terry Alts were a secret rural society formed to hit back at landlords. The ship on which he travelled to Australia was the *Parmelia*. In New South Wales the authorities noted that he was twenty-five years old, married with two children, that he could read and that he had no previous convictions. The general remarks on the New South Wales Convict Rolls say: 'a scar on the back of right hand. Wart on inside middle and fourth fingers of left hand. Scar back of forefinger of left hand. Large scar over inner ankle of right leg.'

After four years attached to work parties, he was assigned to an Australian pastoralist, William Bradley of Braidwood, New South Wales. He served there for eleven years and in 1848 received a conditional pardon, the attached condition being that he should never return to Great Britain or Ireland for the term of his sentence, which of course was life.

My wife's family have a particularly poignant document dated February 1840, and headed, 'The Humble Petition of Esther Larkin. To His Excellency Viscount Elrington, Lord Lieutenant General and General Governor of Ireland'. The petitioner presents herself as a twenty-eight-year-old woman with two children by Hugh Larkin, one ten years old and the other seven. 'Under the above Circumstances, Petr begs of your Excelency to look with the eyes of pity on herself and children and order them a free passage to New South Wales. And Your Excelency's petitioner will forever thankfully pray.'

The letter is signed by three Galway magistrates (one of them John Eyre, whose family gave their name to Galway's town square), who endorse the woman's plea. This petition was denied.

After other appeals from his side had been refused, Hugh Larkin set up house with another ticket-of-leave Irish convict, Mary Shields, a Tipperary kitchenmaid who had been sentenced to seven years at Limerick City in 1838 for stealing 'wearing apparel'. To the peasant or working-class transportee, of course, a seven-year sentence was as good as life. She too had a spouse back in Ireland, and had brought her child, Michael Flynn, with her aboard the *Whitby*. What extraordinary voyages they must have been. The *Whitby*; Master: Thomas Wellbank; John Kidd, Surgeon Superintendent. One hundred and thirty-three female convicts and twenty-three children, of whom only one convict died before the ship landed in Sydney. Surgeon Superintendent John Kidd had made a number of convict voyages and obviously knew his basic, nautical preventative medicine.

When the cathedral of Saints Peter and Paul opened in Goulburn, a town which is fairly close to the site which would become Canberra, the national capital, Hugh Larkin married Mary Shields. That Irish priest who married them in Goulburn must have had some wisdom to regulate the Larkin-Shields ménage and baptise their children. He would have wisely concluded that the distances between Hugh and Esther, between Mary Shields and Mr Flynn, were so absolute as to provide grounds for annulment. Another instance of the fact that while the Irish clergy the world over could take people's breath away with their stodginess, they often bore it away too by their practical compassion.

Larkin and Mary Shields are buried beside each other in Goulburn. But God knows where Esther Tully/Larkin and her children Patrick and Hugh ended their days. Patrick and Hugh are my wife's phantom great-uncles.

\*

When I finished telling this story, the poet tolerantly said, 'Well, of course it is sad. It's *permissible* to feel sad.'

She had given me more than a licence to go ahead indulging myself. Her licence was a validation of a sincere feeling. What better licence-to-feel-a-poignancy could you have than from a woman like this, a baton-carrier for Yeats, a voice from a crevice of the Shannon estuary.

I asked her if she would mind if we dashed off to Coole Park, to the autograph tree where so many Irish writers and artists had signed – George Bernard Shaw, Sean O'Casey, A.E. Even the Welsh painter, Augustus John. All in the demesne of Lady Gregory's estate. Of Lady Gregory, W.B. Yeats said in a letter to Lord Haldane in 1918, 'she knows the country as few know it, and has taken down, for instance, hundreds of thousands of words in collecting folklore from cottage to cottage and has still many ways of learning what is thought about it – is convinced that women and children will stand in front of their men and receive their bullets.' This is in connection with the British plans to conscript the Irish during the Great War.

From here the Widow Gregory, her dead husband, Sir William, a former Governor of Ceylon, had moved out amongst the despised natives, an act which on the face of it might seem a little like a Gauleiter developing an interest in Yiddish theatre, and which most of her social peers had till then managed to resist. And Coole Park became another centre for figures of the pending Irish Revival.

After Coole Park, we came to the plain town of Gort. If you were choosing towns which seemed positioned or built specifically to service the Garrison landowners, Gort would have to be a semi-finalist in its class. And then, through Gort and its water-streaming main street, we reached Thoor Ballylee and the Millhouse Tower, four hundred years old, which Yeats bought for himself and his wife Georgie Hyde-Lees to live and write verse in.

I have been to Yeats's tower twice, and each time a Yeatsian tempest has been blowing as I stood and watched that wonderfully simple, stone-carved poem inset in a slab by the door:

> I, the poet William Yeats,
> With old mill boards and sea-green slates,
> And smithy work from the Gort forge,
> Restored this tower for my wife George;
> And may these characters remain
> When all is ruin once again.

On in age, and in a mood of more complicated pessimism, he wrote 'The Tower':

> What shall I do with this absurdity –
> O heart, O troubled heart – this caricature,
> Decrepit age that has been tied to me
> As to a dog's tail?

The tower served him as an image of love and then of decrepitude. And an image of fatherhood as well. The poet from Ennis looked up to the tower room with an authority which I didn't question, as the mill stream surged past as close to flooding the tower as ever it had come in its long history. 'He wrote the "Prayer For My Daughter" up there,' she said. 'Behind that window.'

36

And of course the opening lines lend credence to it:

> Once more the storm is howling, and half hid
> Under this cradle-hood and coverlid
> My child sleeps on. There is no obstacle
> But Gregory's wood and one bare hill
> Whereby the haystack – and roof-levelling wind,
> Bred on the Atlantic, can be stayed;
> And for an hour I have walked and prayed
> Because of the great gloom that is in my mind.
>
> I have walked and prayed for this young child an hour
> And heard the sea-wind scream upon the tower,
> And under the arches at the bridge, and scream
> In the elms above the flooded stream;

On the day I was there with the poet from Ennis, future years were certainly coming, dancing to the beating of a frenzied drum, 'out of the murderous innocence' of the Atlantic. And the locked tower seemed an appropriate venue for the ghosts of the extraordinary Yeats couple, William frowning, fretting about daughters and Ireland, and fey Mrs Yeats – Georgie – in contact with the spirit world, doing her pages and pages of automatic writing here, giving her husband thereby the framework for *The Vision*.

'I've been here at least a dozen times,' the red-haired poet told me functionally. There was an implication that she loved Yeats in an habitual sort of way, that this was just another visit and not a pilgrimage. There was the heady chance that there might come to be structures from her own background, incorporated in her own writing, worth a visit one day.

She praised the Yeats sites further north in Sligo. Later I would visit them. The country around Ballisodare and Lissadell House, Constance Markiewicz's childhood home, is laced with beautiful coastal and hillside roads called The Yeats Way, which must pulsate with Yeats lovers in the summer but which in autumn yields only the occasional neckerchiefed farmer. Great Ben Bulben, where the Celtic Achilles Diarmuid died when a wild boar's bristles punctured his heel, dominates the coast of Yeats country. Here Yeats wanted to be buried, and he wrote his own obituary in 1938 in 'Under Ben Bulben':

> Under bare Ben Bulben's head
> In Drumcliff churchyard Yeats is laid,
> An ancestor was rector there
> Long years ago; a church stands near,
> By the road an ancient Cross.
> No marble, no conventional phrase,
> On limestone quarried near the spot
> By his command these words are cut:
> Cast a cold eye
> On life, on death. Horseman, pass by!

Born under a different star of sensibility, Ezra Pound parodied this late poem:

> Neath Ben Bulben's buttoks lies
> Bill Yeats, a poet twoice the soize
> Of William Shakespear, as they say
> Down Ballykillywuchlin way.

Though good friends, Pound probably hated Yeats's Irish sensuality, the letting-down-of-the-team aspects of one of Yeats's last poems, written on the eve of the Second World War:

> How can I, that girl standing there,
> My attention fix
> On Roman or on Russian
> Or on Spanish politics . . .
> But O that I were young again
> And held her in my arms.

Because he died in the south of France, Yeats's body wasn't returned to the lovely churchyard of Drumcliff, by St Columba's standing cross, until 1948. He lies on the north side of the church, under Ben Bulben's grey bulk. The stone reads as he prescribed:

Horseman, pass by!

# FIVE

I have been to Inishmore, the main Aran Isle, and seen the extraordinary cliffs on the south-west side, the semi-circular pre-Christian fortress of Dun Aengus which is built right up to the cliff. The Aran Isle ferry leaves from the Galway coast at Rossaveel, the Inishmaan one from Spidal. Both these ports are at the base of the triangle of great peat bog which they call Iar Connacht. I'm not sure what *Iar* means. Probably desolation. Although the Irish may not look upon peat bogs as desolations. More as bounties.

I had always believed, the one time I went to Inishmore, that I was seeing the ultimate Celts. That was the message I had seemed to pick up from J.M. Synge's *Riders To the Sea* which I'd had to study in high school in Australia. From that text, I think even the crassest of us got an idea of a sweet, brave, lost Celtic world.

A sea-going Celtic world too. And there are the black, tarry currachs leaned against the sea wall at Kilronan and Kilmurvey. You'll even see the occasional currach sitting off one of Inishmore's beautiful beaches, or else – as implied by Synge's plays – making off for Inishmaan. Riding to the sea. St Brendan, putative discoverer of America and hero of all seagoing Irish, is buried on rocky Inishmore, this island which looks like a calf of the stony Burren.

Add to these impressions of Celtichood, the news of how the Land Leaguers in the nineteenth century would drive rackrenting landlords' cattle over the enormous cliffs of Aran, and how Republicans sheltered there during the War of Independence, and listen then to the ubiquitous Gaelic of the place, and you might conclude that Aran was a focus of lost Irishness.

Ireland both accommodates and makes a mock of that sort of conclusion. And good Anglo-Irish gents like Synge, in their enthusiasm, added to the confusion. For now historians are telling us that the slab-browed, dour, dark face of the Aran islanders comes as much from the soldiers of Cromwell who were stationed on the islands, who stayed on after Cromwell's death and the return of Charles II, who bespoke the local girls, who took on the despised tongue and the despised religion, and whose descendants became the adored Gaels of Douglas Hyde's Gaelic Revival, and a source of study for Synge, who lived on Inishmaan and Inishmore for some two years.

This journey, I had a mandate to go to the more northerly islands off the Connemara Coast: Inishbofin and Inishturk. The furthest out of all. I knew that relatives of Paddy Prendergast lived on Inishturk. I had seen Paddy's photographs of their currachs, and of the wind-bullied graveyard there, where the grave decorations have to be tethered down with stones or wire, the little glass domes of artificial flowers held in place by fringes of cricket ball-sized stones to stop them flying into the sea.

All the guidebooks say that your passage to Inishbofin and Inishturk is dependent on weather. I waited at Letterfrack, at Rosleague Manor, a wonderful nineteenth-century house run in an individual style by a family called Foyle and hung with contemporary pictures of the Galway gentry and Connemara scenes. Each day I called the pub at Cleggan. 'I'll just go and have a look at the water,' the publican would say, put the phone down, go to the window, consider the fury of the Atlantic, return and say, 'It's nothing but white caps. No boat from Inishbofin or Inishturk today.'

It was six days, in fact, since one had come.

41

*

I said goodbye to the genial Foyles, brother and sister, who run Rosleague, and went up to Renvyle House, on a peninsula facing the sea, for dinner. I met up with an Irish public servant and his wife and mother-in-law, and we sat there, in a gale as absolute as anything in Yeats's poetry, trading tales of what we knew of the place. Renvyle House had belonged to Oliver St John Gogarty, the surgeon and author of *As I Was Walking Down Sackville Street*. He invited literary folk out here, but one who didn't come was Joyce. Joyce, however, transmuted him into the 'stately, plump' Buck Mulligan who opens *Ulysses*, standing blasphemously on the tower south of Dun Laoghaire with his enamel basin of shaving water. He had 'a finical sweet voice' and blinked his eyes pleasantly, if the depiction of the Buck is anything to go by. He was also a cadger and a jovial exploiter, conning Stephen Daedalus out of his money and the key to the tower.

In real life, he earned enough to buy Renvyle. Cork and the West of Ireland remained very Republican even after the establishment of the Irish Free State, and Connemara Republicans of the 4th Western Division of the IRA, in rebellion against the Free State forces led by Michael Collins, burned Gogarty's Renvyle down in that bitter, fraternal mayhem of the early 20s (Gogarty rebuilt it with British Government compensation – Sir Edwin Lutyens was the architect – it was rebuilt and reopened by Gogarty as an hotel in 1930).

On the dark way back to Letterfrack that night, I took the wrong turn, and found myself taking the long road home, between the god-awesome Twelve Bens on one side, the Maumturk Mountains on the other. Their layers of rock glistened weirdly with water in the moonlight and Loch Inagh surged like a sea beside the road. This was like the

Burren; this too was the last of Ireland, the bit the O'Flahertys kept for themselves, that terrible tribe of O'Flahertys who were commemorated on the old city gates of Galway in the tag: 'From the fury of the O'Flahertys, good Lord deliver us.' A wild night in the circle from Letterfrack to Recess to sleeping Clifden, which has seen all the sorrows, and back to Letterfrack, that good Quaker settlement of the nineteenth century which seems to have gone utterly native. With no other headlight to prove that the world hasn't stopped, I edged through the gears amongst those great deities of mountains, and was literally sobered, though the Irish public servant had been generous with cordials and infusions.

It is possible for a normal, that is neurotic, human to fear the threat of annihilation in certain landscapes. They are often bare and barren landscapes – the Olgas, a primeval set of mountains west of Ayers Rock in Central Australia; Arches or Canyonlands National Park in Utah where there's so much naked space that you cling to the steering wheel expecting nullity to strike just around the next curve. A Scotswoman I met would deny that the Twelve Bens were awesome – 'We've got bigger hills at home,' she said. She was talking about the Coolins of the Isle of Skye.

But it is never just a matter of scale. It is a matter of a kind of intensity too, and of primeval presence. You don't feel it in the Rockies because they're so damned pretty. Whereas at midnight, in a lull in a gale, the Twelve Bens are not trying to please anyone but themselves. They are secure and indifferent in their unbeatable Ben-ness. If my vehicle had had a creep gear, I would have slid into it, as the lough water splashed up across the highway and the Bens and the Maums pended down upon my sense of identity. I knew too, as a not-so-good Catholic with a schooled sense of what heresy is, and how close it is to orthodoxy, that this feeling was the beginning of animism and of the religion of place, of holy wells and of consecrated mountains like Croagh Patrick, which dressed up in Aves and Pater Nosters and Glory Be's and seven times circling of certain rocks and certain wells, is so dominant a part of Irish observance.

The next day being one of horizontal water borne on the gale, the publican at Cleggan being again able only to see mists and rearing white caps, I said goodbye to the Foyles a last time, standing in their house where all was grand except the entry hall, a companionable little entry way under all those faces captured in oils. Now I made my way round the coast to Cashla Bay, in English the bay of the fort. There was another fine house there, the McEvillys' Cashel House Hotel, an old home socketed into the narrow, green seaside hills rimming the immensities of peat.

I stopped on the way in high-steepled Clifden, a town savaged by the Black and Tans, riven in the Civil War, plagued still by emigration, hard-core Irish trying to be a seaside spa.

Given that Connemara harbours illicit stills where the colourless alcohol *poitin* (potcheen) is distilled from potatoes, someone suggested it might be worth talking to a Garda about the stuff. For the gale that was blowing was blowing in the right season, October, the end of the potato harvest, after which the making of the liquor in secret stills begins. I went to the Garda station on the north side of Clifden and introduced myself. The experience of Australians in Ireland, particularly in the West, is that first they are presumed to be English – probably Cockney, speaking not in the accents of the oppressor, but in the accents of the armies of the oppressor. Then it's discovered that you are Australian, and then that you have Irish connections. This is the daily estrangement and homecoming which an Australian experiences in Ireland. Suspicion replaced by regard, replaced then by warmth. It was so with every person I picked up on the side of the road, and it was so in the Garda station, which was manned that morning by a young, lantern-jawed cop.

The Garda uniform is a nineteenth-century design, devised to make raw-boned, lantern-jawed boys like this look gawky. But his suspicion was precise when I first asked the question. No, no, there was no problem with *poitin* in Clifden. Oh sure, it was made elsewhere in Connemara. In South Connemara, and along the coast say between Rossaveel and Galway, there was a lot of trading in it. Trading between the coast and the Arans. Connemara, he admitted then, and the islands were the main centres of production. But I should talk to the Garda in Oughterard, who were – according to what he knew – arresting *poitin* distillers and smugglers regularly. Mind you, he confessed, there had been a big arrest in the Clifden area – a man who was depoting stuff distilled elsewhere and selling it. The longer the policeman talked, the more enthusiastic he became about the properties of *poitin*, about the true distillation and the true distillers. The old makers were very good at it, he said. They produced a pure product, clear as glass, safe to consume in moderation – two tumblers would see a man through heartbreak or pneumonia. 'No,' he said, 'you couldn't take more than two tumblers. You'd start to do yourself a damage.' Now for congestive ailments, he told me, because the stuff had such a powerful proof, one hundred and sixty or more, it was wonderful with hot water and lemon. And if you pulled a muscle or a joint, it was a superb lineament. I asked him about the price, and he said that it was four to five punts, as compared to whisky at fourteen punts a bottle. I don't want to imply that he was Flann O'Brien's comic Garda, but the Gardaí come from the people too, even though old Nationalists despise and mistrust them. As Ulick O'Connor writes, 'As a boy I could never understand why my father, a courteous man, could be abrupt with policemen. When confronted by the Garda Siochana he became terse. His voice snapped if he had been driving his car, and they wished him goodbye. He often observed that if you notice something peculiar in a man's eye, if he wouldn't look straight at you, it would nearly always turn out he was the son of a policeman.'

Despite such a hard judgement, this boy in Clifden was of somewhere in the West, and knew ancestrally of the benefits of the stuff, even if it was proscribed by statute.

You could tell this by the way he spoke with true venom about the young, opportunistic distillers who had come into the business for quick money, and not with a dedication to the craft. They were the true criminals as distinct from the merely technical and traditional lawbreakers. He had no inhibitions about cracking down on them.

I thought of how the tradition had been transplanted to the mountains of Appalachia, how in the coal miners' strike of 1978, the bottled lightning, clear as electricity, was passed around in jars to fortify another struggle and another misery in another place.

The hills of Connemara therefore, so exquisite, so austere, have historically concealed and still conceal a number of stills. This is the landscape of 'To hell or Connaught', to quote Cromwell's prescription for dealing with the native Irish by reducing them to barbarians in Ireland's poorest portion. Here life, even two generations ago, was unutterably primitive and stripped to the bone. How important then *poitín* must have been not just as a soother but as a healer. 'Oh yes,' said another old farmer of whom I asked the question in a bar in Leenane. 'In the great influenza epidemic after *that* war, lots more people would have died without it.'

\*

Another interesting thing the Garda had told me in Clifden as I idled out the gale was that Gardaí can't be appointed to their own area. They have to come from at least fifty miles away, that is, from a whole new network of fealties. Fifty miles is still a long way out here in the West.

When you look at the new housing estates of Wexford or Galway or Limerick, you wonder if tribalism will be sapped of its blood in these rows of bungalows, so that as in most nations, people within an acre's radius are strangers to each other, and any cop can be allocated to police them because everyone is equally estranged. Maybe. The cities of Ulster would seem to say that tribalism is in the bone. But, of course, there are other forces at work up there in the north, forces which do not work in a new suburb of a provincial city in the Republic.

The Garda's mention of a fifty-mile limit reminded me of a police incident in the deserts of Central Australia, where some action had to be taken over petrol sniffing by tribal adolescents. The Aboriginal policeman involved came from three hundred miles away, in South Australia. In the dry deserts of the Centre, three hundred miles was tribally the equivalent of fifty miles in Connemara.

At Cashel House on Galway's south coast, in the midst of the desert of peat, I ate more fine dinners on behalf of my grandmother, and listened Yeats-like to the gale, nonetheless setting out every morning dutifully to travel amongst the peat bogs and the mountains and talk with people. And the weather began to clear up down here, in this bare, brutal country, this country full of interest but devoid of obvious merit, the sort of landscape which prepared the Irish well for the New World, for California, Australia, the plains of Canada. The country, too, in which Pearse, the mystic of revolution, kept a hut and wrote his uncomplicated revolutionary poetry, pledging his blood for Ireland's redemption – a curious business for the son of an English sculptor – but Ireland produces such exorbitant effects in the spirit.

47

*

I gave a lift one day to a sturdy and informative young woman who emerged from a laneway on the east side of Clifden. After running through, as if it were required, the glories of Clifden, including the annual Connemara Pony Show, to which Peter O'Toole comes – she had drunk champagne at the Pony Show with Peter O'Toole; she was handsome enough for that – she told me about the laneway from which she had emerged. The Black and Tans, British police auxiliaries brought in to control the Irish countryside in 1920 and, given that there were not enough bottle-green uniforms to go round, equipped with surplus khaki, were strong and most dangerous in the West here. This girl's grandmother was ninety years old and still alive and remembered it all and had passed it on. Even if the facts were garbled, the import would have been exact. The story, secondhand through this young woman, was that the Black and Tans in Clifden required that if you lived in town you had a picture of the monarch on your wall. On Sundays, they cordoned off the church, where these days the parish priest's main concern is that motorists from the EC or the US will park all over the space in front of the church and block out the worshippers.

People of Clifden, therefore, came out here in 1920 to this laneway and built a shanty town. Then the Black and Tans visited and put it to the torch.

The woman, who was studying nursing in Galway city, told me her own family had stayed on at the little settlement, after the burning, and had built a more permanent structure there. But she confessed she would probably end up in England anyhow, working as a nurse. The grand-daughters of the defiant women of the West bound to the economy, the opportunity of England.

Like any Irish passenger, she gave me two gifts: her own

48

rich story, and someone else's preposterous one. Amongst the bare bends, we passed a National School house. She told me that the local people refused to send their children there. They disapproved of the teacher's methods in the broad sense. The teacher was said to intrude into the children's lives too much – whatever that means in Connemara. The government wouldn't withdraw her, and so for four years, she has – even as I write – opened the school every day, and has sat down at the desk in front of an utterly empty classroom. It is hard for me to predict what lonely convictions drive her. What communal convictions drive the parents, it is likewise hard for me to say.

*

At last there was a clear morning. I went up to Cleggan, and found that the Inishbofin boat, a converted trawler ill-maintained, had just come in. I ran down to the wharf and discovered, already aboard, an English honeymoon couple, having an eccentric honeymoon indeed by English standards – no snorkelling in the Maldives. They too were the only people with an obsession to get to Inishbofin that day of the storm's tail. Apart, of course, from four plasterers and painters from Mayo, who had been waiting some days to make the crossing so that they could work on Inishbofin's fanciest building, of which I would learn a little more later. And there was a wife too, the youngish wife of someone on Inishbofin. She'd been shopping, I'd supposed, probably wrongly. Later I'd find out that an Islander had recently married an Englishwoman in Bath, and lots of Inishbofin people had gone over for the nuptials, and some were still straggling home.

Loaves of Brennan's bread and mail and eight days' worth of the *Irish Times* and the *Irish Press* were the cargo.

We were about to take off when an eccentric ship, painted

orange and black, came in and sought to run a rope across our bows. I should have known that this was the Inishturk boat, the first one for a week. I didn't. And so we put off across the narrow and stormy passage, leaving the red and black ship behind. And I thought, as I talked to the plasterers who were working on a German house on the island, this was but the start of St Brendan's voyage, and this craft is many times greater and more seaworthy than Brendan's. And the Atlantic, on a day like this, is so enormous, even when Inishbofin lies offshore to take the brunt.

Soon after leaving Cleggan, you could see Inishbofin growing to the west. And then it grew further, and its long, right-turn harbour reached for us.

If the Burren seemed an appropriate landscape for monasticism, all the more so does Inishbofin. St Colmán, the same St Colmán who made a foundation down in Cloyne, came here from Lindisfarne after he had been expelled by the Synod of Whitby in 664 over a question as crucial as the date of Easter. Colmán, who must have been an individualist, brought forty English monks with him to Inishbofin, and somehow recruited Irish monks as well.

The English honeymoon couple, and the plasterers and painters and I, arrived in the main harbour of Inishbofin, its sixteenth- or seventeenth-century ruined fort off to one side, its pared-down town on the other.

I walked up through the few streets of the port and tried to see Inishbofin as a centre of seventh-century enthusiasm. It must have been magnetic, something like Southern California, to draw the crowds of devotees it did. To generate the activity. For there was a conflict among the monks, the Irish and the others – I don't know whether over theology or calendar or both – but to save a schism Colmán moved half the establishment ashore to Mayo, and then presided over both places.

St Columba/Columbkille himself wrote in the sixth century of places like this:

> On some island I long to be,
> a rocky promontory, looking on
> the coiling surface of the sea.
> To see the waves, crest on crest
> of the great shining ocean, composing
> a hymn to the creator, without rest . . .

Inishbofin means the Island of the White Cow.

Every island has its mythology. The mythology of the Aran Isles, for instance, includes the claim that a further isle is seen offshore. Its name is Hy Brasil, and it is the Isle of Heart's Content. The idyll of Inishbofin involves an old woman who was sighted by two fishermen driving a white cow along the beach, perhaps the very beach called Horseshoe Bay, the harbour beach of the island. Hitting it with a stick, she was turned to stone, and the two fisherman hit her and were also turned to stone. They are visible on the shore. A viable basis for an island; out of which the white cow survived.

On Inishbofin, when a girl marries, her father supplies a white cow as her marriage portion. That still happens. The bovine dowry.

\*

Apart from the retriever dog who meets the boat, and knowing you want to hire a bike, accompanies you north along the island's spine to the bike-hiring cottage, there are no distractions on Inishbofin. The Atlantic's salt breath has kept the island bare of trees. There are no distractions in Inishbofin, especially from September onwards. And few distractions for the eye, though the island is quite large. Sea, stone, the line of the low hills are all the elements to be concentrated upon. An island built for the contemplation of absolutes.

It defeats the imagination. Could there have been raging monks in this place? How were they drawn here? Some of them Italians, some of them English, and then the local boys? How were they drawn, and how was the message spread throughout the British Isles that here, on an island off Connemara, was the centre of sensibility, the key to existence? What made someone from the mainstream of Europe decide – in the middle of the seventh century – that Inishbofin, the furthest island out, was the essential environment? And yet that was the way it worked: Hollywood had no greater pull in the 1930s than the Atlantic islands in their high day. All without radio and the printing press to spread the message. How astonishing.

Now the island has a population of fishermen and dairy farmers and their families. The fishermen operate both in the larger boats and in the smaller traditional currachs, an outboard motor attached to their sterns. Currachs follow an ancient design. They sit very low in the water, they are straight for most of their length, they have a long bow with narrow gunnels on top. Their prows are suddenly pointed. It all must work, since it seems that people like the Prendergasts and the Concannons of Inishturk have been fishing from such vessels for the better part of a millennium. Their local knowledge must balance out the apparent flimsiness of their black-bowed craft. They must be privy to every variation of wind and current, to every possibility of fury, between Inishturk, Inishbofin and the mainland.

So are these people Celts, or what are they? There's no doubt that some of them have a Viking look, and there can be little question that these must have been much favoured and easily secured bases for the Norsemen, who might have been charming in quieter moments, and might have had a line of palaver of their own, etcetera, etcetera.

'See you at five on the beach,' the captain had told us as we came ashore in the dinghy. There are obviously few deep anchorages in Inishbofin's narrow harbour.

I hired a bike and set off discreetly, in an opposite direction to the English honeymooners. They would never forget their being on Inishbofin. Whereas I was here for the day.

On a bike with gears, but otherwise worthy of celebration by Flann O'Brien, I bumped downhill through a flock of sheep, and uphill to the cemetery.

Inishbofin didn't have funerary monuments before about 1890. Before that, mounds marked out by stones would have been the only markers. If there were wooden crosses, how quickly the wind would have dealt with them.

The gravestones of Inishbofin, therefore, have all been constructed on the mainland and brought over on the converted trawler, dropped into a currach, and rowed ashore. And the names on these memorial stones seemed to favour certain clans: the Alleys, the Lavelles, Laceys, Concannons, Burkes, Coynes. The gravestones generally record which quarter of the island the deceased comes from. 'Middlequarter', 'Westquarter', 'Eastquarter'. It was as if the quarter other than the one they had derived from had been populated by miscreants of the same name, with whom the deceased did not wish to be mistaken. There is one woman in the graveyard of whom her gravestone boasts, 'The whole island grieves her loss.'

That rare statement goes unassailed still, on the face of the stone and in the face of the wind.

*

Yet again, what a shame it was that after the penal laws were suspended and the native Irish began rebuilding their churches, they didn't have a closer look at the days of Colmán and his monks, or at the Romanesque days. There is an ugly Catholic church on the island, overlooking the harbour. Just like the one in Cloyne, it is named after St Colmán. It is only on the inside that it is alive and wonderful, the archetypal Irish church, the church you can find everywhere from the Yukon to Tasmania. For this church on an Atlantic island has what the churches of Ireland lack – a populated feel. I do not mean to imply for a moment that the Church of Ireland has not bravely and robustly dealt with its existence on the Irish mainland, or that its worshippers have not been forthright and estimable people. But its speciality is the great exterior and the cold interior. With the native Irish it's the other way round: the crass exterior, the vibrant interior. Or is this just a matter of the burning sanctuary lamp – according to my childhood teaching, the sign that *God Is In*.

I confess that I was *In*, in part, for shelter from the relentless wind which polishes and combs the island all day and all night. And while in, I noticed that by the prie-dieu to one side of the altar are the framed photographs of five twentieth-century Inishbofin boys who had been ordained priests and gone to foreign missions and died there. They were Laceys and Lavelles, and had perished in China, Liberia, Nigeria. I couldn't help wondering what it was Inishbofin had given them – the perilous currach fishing, the garnering of meat from the seals which come up on the rocks beneath the cliffs on the west side of the island, the milking of white cows, the unremitting voice of the wind – which they felt they had at any cost, even at the cost of life, to pass on to the Chinese and the Africans.

For their folk fished and herded cows on Europe's last tier of rock. They were impelled, just the same, to take Europe's message. From the third world of Inishbofin to the Third World proper. One thing: they would have understood the Africans and the Cantonese as few city-bred priests would have. They would have understood the subsistence peasant.

They belonged to an order called the Columbans, named after Columbkille or Columba of Iona, as distinct from the slightly later Colmán or Columbanus, the one who founded the turbulent monastery on Inishbofin in the seventh century.

In the porch of the church is a history of the Columbans, the elite corps in which the Lavelles and Laceys of Inishbofin had perished. The order was founded by a Maynooth professor, a sure bet for a bishopric, named John Blowick. 'John Blowick's father had bought his ticket to emigrate to Australia; he was to leave the family's thatched cottage in Belcarra, County Mayo, to make way for his older brother who had just married, and who would be taking over the farm.'

(This is what we are, I thought, the Australians, a nation of non-inheritors of the farm.)

'One snowy January morning in 1867 the newlyweds were found suffocated. Because of the bitter cold they had brought a bucket of hot coals into their unventilated room. So Johnny Blowick cancelled his journey to Australia and stayed on in Belcarra to work the land.'

And his son became founder of the Columbans amongst whom the Inishbofin boys served. With young Johnny Blowick, star pupil and then professor at Maynooth as with St Francis, there was a St Clare: the widowed Lady Maloney, who formed the Missionary Sisters of Saint Columban. If any Inishbofin girl joined them, taking on their black habit with the indented coif (how would that have been on a hot day in Shanghai, in the seasons of cholera?), their photographs aren't in the sanctuary of the Inishbofin church.

As I mentioned, on the way over on the trawler, there had been a number of young painters and plasterers from Westport in Mayo's southern corner. They were crossing to work on the house of a German, who had acquired a little land on the island and was building his own version of a European outpost, a stonehouse with a tower. The Islanders and even the men from Westport exhibited a quite daunting, amused tolerance for the idea. This seems to be the pervasive attitude of the Western Irish to anyone who tries to find a haven amongst them. It is as if they were saying, Groucho Marx-wise, that they couldn't respect anyone who chose their destiny, to live in Connaught or its offshore rocks.

Later in the day, biking between Westquarter and the cliffs on the island's far side, I passed the German's house, stone, as the workmen had promised, and a little circular tower, nothing ridiculous, the expression of a man who feels for the place and understands its steeple-toppling winds. The Islanders said he was a German restaurateur. Surely in the seventh century his impulses would have made him a monk.

By a little lake on the east side of the island, a low place which the more furious winds would probably bounce across, stand the stones of a medieval church by a shore of reeds (a possible source of paper for Colmán's monks). It is believed to stand on the site where Colmán founded his monastery in the 660s. His vote against the Roman method of calculating the date of Easter, registered in 663 or 664, like most decisions of the time which look like a matter of indifference now, must have had all manner of theological, political, philosophical cargo attached to it.

Again, he brought to Inishbofin (how had he heard of it?) all the Irish monks of Lindisfarne and some thirty English ones. How to reconstruct their enthusiasm out of this bare vale? And then, when there was further ideological trouble in the monastery of Inishbofin, he took the English party ashore to Mayo, and planted them there, at Bangor. It is probably best not to think about the minute, unstable skin-covered craft in which all these passionate departures were made.

It is the testing impulse of God which sets up an immensity like the Atlantic and a consistency like a west wind. It is the mercy of God to provide such a cunning and neatly slotted corridor of harbour as this. There, by the water, on the east side of the haven, by what was Cromwell's star-shaped fort and attendant gulag for Catholic clerics from the mainland, is a rock called Bishop's Rock, where a bishop was tethered by Cromwellian troops, who then watched the tide come in and drown his papism. Again, God knows how that Inishbofin death in the seventeenth century compelled the Fathers Lacey and Lavelle to their African and Chinese deaths.

Apart from monasticism and enthusiasm, what is there to sustain the average Islander? 'What do most of the fellas in Inishbofin do?' I asked the captain of the trawler-ferry.

And he replied, 'Fook-all'.

*

Cromwell's fortress, whose rooms still stand there, on the side of the harbour across from the town called Middlequarter, has incorporated an edifice named Bosco's Tower. Bosco was a Spaniard, a freebooter who worked with the renowned sixteenth-century privateering chieftainess and widow named Grainne Ni Mhaille, Grace O'Malley. She was the daughter of O'Malley, Lord of Upper Umhall, and she typified the way the Irish chiefs got on with the English, cosseting them, and being used in return. Born in 1530, in 1574 she beat off an English seaboard expedition against Carraig Castle on Achill Island. In 1577, she was captured by the Earl of Desmond and imprisoned in Limerick and Dublin, and persuaded to work against her rebel husband, Richard, forefather of some of the Burkes who lie in Inishbofin graveyard. Late in the sixteenth century, she appeared before Elizabeth I to ask that her licence to 'harry the Queen's enemies with fire and sword' should not be revoked. At this stage of history, she was in her late sixties, a fire-eater then, an iron-maiden. She was called 'the sea-queen'. She has, of course, become mythologised, like Maire Rua. Her legends stretch from this side of Eire to the other. The St Lawrence family of Howth in Dublin always set an extra place at table because of Grace O'Malley, who came to the gate of Howth Castle one day to discover that it was locked and closed for dinner. In vengeance, she carried off the

St Lawrence heir and let him be ransomed only on the promise that the castle never again close its gate at dinner time.

You find traces of the great Grace all along the West coast. She is an island-spanning deity. A base on Inishbofin would have given her a fierce control over the trade along the West coast. Though her name was soft, her trade was hard.

*

On the banks of Lough Mask, the autumnal gale was still blowing. As on Inishbofin, simple elements made up heaven and earth: driving clouds kept level with the mountaintops, which were stony and deep green and ran white threads of the season's water down their faces. Lower down were the peaty flanks, where the black stacks of peat sod waited beside the trenches from which they had been cut. And there was a house on its own, again one of Ireland's new, brick and white-stucco farm houses, an EC special, the successor to the white-limed and sod-roofed version which most people still imagine when they think of rural Ireland, certainly of the Ireland of their ancestors.

I'd seen many such houses in desolate places, sometimes the only house in sight, the only trite human gesture in a potent scene. And there had always been something strange about these new farmhouses of Ireland and, driving up Lough Mask, I understood what it was. Blinds and drapes had not been pulled across the window, even part way, as you would expect people to do to keep the warmth in on such a day. The picture windows stared full and frank and uncovered into the face of the wind, and at the sides, lace curtains showed trimly. Only the hurricane spoke and the sun was blinded with thick cloud, but the lace was on display.

In the diaspora, again, the term 'lace-curtain Irish' is pejorative. It could mean someone of Irish descent who was trying to forget or cover his origins.

I have actually heard the term used about the fine Irish-American writer John Gregory Dunn, who according to the speaker's perspective, had the good or ill fortune to come from a well-to-do Irish-American family in Connecticut. The argument was that this somehow disqualified him from writing books such as *True Confessions* and even *Harp*, from telling tales about poor Irish-Americans who grow up to be lawyers or monsignors.

And so, there was obviously a time in Ireland itself when lace curtains might have stood for some sort of treachery, some selling out, some surrender to the Garrison. That perception obviously travelled with the emigrants of an earlier time, went to distant places and became a dogma.

But not in Ireland itself. As the rain slants down on Partree, as it flails the *Gaeltacht* (Gaelic-speaking area) in Mayo, you'll see in the vacant windows the white lace, ruched and scalloped and immaculate behind the glass. The women of Ireland, you feel, have been waiting a long time for their lace curtains, through a millennium of turmoils, bitter farewells, treacheries, dispositions and bereavement. Now the lace says for them, 'We're doing all right, thank you. Nice. Nice lace. Behind the gale-proof armour glass. Send us your tornadoes and we'll put some trimming on them and hem them to our purposes.' That's how well things are by the lough, beneath the mountain in the Republic of Ireland in the European Community.

Amidst the peat fields, where rain lies smirking in the black trenches, the lace smiles wholesomely.

\*

It's hard to see how Ireland could have reached its 1841 population of over eight million and sustained itself since without its peat bogs. In the old song, 'A Bowl of Punch', a good peat or 'turf' fire is counted an equal blessing to a lass and a glass. We're told the boglands have been foolishly drained, and therefore Ireland's great resource is diminishing.

It is fascinating to be instructed by locals in what made the peat. Ireland's trees fell into the shallow fens caused by the melting of an ice cap, and lying there they began the process of becoming coal and of impregnating the soil with their carbon. There are still Irish doorways – in pubs and old farmhouses – which have black logs as lintels, four or five millennia old that had been dug up from the local bog.

Men cut the peat out of long, shallow trenches, whose black sides are fluted neatly by the action of the peat shovel, the loy, the kind with which Christy, Synge's *Playboy of the Western World*, claims in the play to have killed his father. Peat is carefully 'footed' in mounds, so it can shed the water with which it is clogged. In many parts of Ireland, where the peat is deep-lying, it is industrially dug. But you still come across men digging it on a co-operative basis.

It is the drowned forest of ready fuel without which life in this moist, windy island could not have been supported.

The traveller thinks the digging of peat is quite picturesque, and is of course disappointed to come across the occasional mechanical digger. You should not, however, presume to take pictures of men digging peat or bearing it down to the road in creels. I did it once in Galway, thinking the normal guff: *this is how our ancestors really lived*. I had my wife with me, and my two young daughters. One of them had recently been enchanted by the book *Peter Pan* and was very concerned to be assured that Peter existed. She would not be put off with such cynical or glib answers as: 'If you believe he exists, then he does', or, 'Of course he exists. He exists in our imaginations.' As I took a picture of the peat diggers, she was asking the question again, the eternal question: 'Does Peter really live?' Does the heart's desire have flesh? A big raw man with a creel and a shovel was advancing on me, yelling, 'Don't you have any fooking manners?' Meanwhile my daughter was asking the other question, 'Yes, but does he really exist?' The answer to both questions, hers and the peat digger's, was of course, 'No.'

Anyhow, I got back into the car with my family and drove away without answering the man or giving him a chance to hit me, something of which I've always been ashamed. Mentally, I use the children as my excuse. It wouldn't have been good for them to see their father pushed around or hit with a loy. It wouldn't have been good for their father either.

In discussing peat, they tell us to think of Ireland as a bowl, the sides of the bowl are the coastal mountains. The middle is the boglands and the peat. This does not quite explain to a layman like me why peat grows all the way up to the side of the Atlantic on, say, the Curraun Peninsula in Mayo, or why it is so visible in Connemara, Donegal and Mayo, the bowl's edges. More understandable are the layers: the sphagnum moss on top of the peat – this upper layer was used for sod roofing till recently. The peat proper beneath it; and then below the peat itself, a limey fertiliser.

What a wonderful source the peat bog was to the Irish: roof and warmth and an inducement to crops. Peat as the preserver. But murder if set alight – the peat bogs of Mayo carry roadside signs begging that care be taken not to start a fire.

The peat is not only Ireland's dearest resource. It is Ireland's depository. I think of those wonderful poems of Seamus Heaney. To him the bog is Ireland's imagination, waiting to be turned over with a spade:

> To lift the lid of the peat
> And find this pupil dreaming
> Of neolithic wheat!
> When he stripped off blanket bog
> The soft-piled centuries

Fell open like a glib:
There were the first plough-marks,
The stone-age fields, the tomb
Corbelled, turfed and chambered,
Floored with dry turf-coomb . . .

Out of the bog appear these brave farms, appear grindstones and canoes, beads and the noble gold and silver ornaments. How the dead rise on the given day from the bog:

. . . barbered
and stripped by a turfcutter's spade . . .

They found a shaven-haired 'little adulteress' in a peat bog in Donegal, not far – as Heaney lets you know in his poem 'Punishment' – from where in Derry other Irish women suffered for choosing the inappropriate man:

. . . your betraying sisters,
cauled in tar,
wept by the railings . . .

As the blood laws can be violated in Derry, so were they violated in neolithic Ireland, and the record of punishment was deposited in the bog:

Murdered, forgotten, nameless, terrible
Beheaded girl, outstaring axe,
And beatification . . .

The peat bog delivers everything up, the gold and silver utterly untainted, the human sacrifices cured and perfect:

Who will say 'corpse'
to his vivid cast?
Who will say 'body'
to his opaque repose?

*Ireland: The Rough Guide* tells me that bogland is shrinking by eight thousand acres a year, yet to the traveller in rural Ireland peat seems everywhere stacked and covered with plastic bags, like someone's shopping left out in the rain. Conservationists are concerned with the quantity of industrially dug turf being exported to the continent by Bord na Mona – the government body which administers this natural resource.

But, when all the other fuels are gone, it is to be hoped that the peat bogs – fed with fresh pine trees – will still supply the Irish.

# SIX

The first time I ever went to Ireland, people warned me about the tinkers. 'One will offer to tell your fortune, while another takes your hubcaps. Or the luggage out of your boot.'

Even in the mid-'70s, when we stayed in the farmhouses and when I showed such poor form on the edge of a peat bog in Galway, the variously named tinkers and gypsies still lived in horse-drawn caravans. These days you can rent that sort of conveyance out to take slow holidays down Ireland's lanes. (The tinkers took their name from their origins as tinsmiths but have now moved on to other crafts and more modern vehicles.)

The Irish give the tinkers great credit for preternatural craftiness and also for charm. The boy or girl of good stock who is enchanted by a gypsy is one of the staples of Irish folksong and popular literature.

'There's the blood in young Donnelly,' a girl sings in one such song of a tinker:

> There's the blood in bold Donnelly,
> He's the boy for me!

In *The Field* too, both the play and film, Bull McCabe's son courts ruin in the arms of a tinker girl. Tinkers, goes the message, emanate a perilous sexuality, dangerous and an affront to decency.

All this would seem to mean that the Irish don't quite

know what to do with their tinkers. They are the aborigines of Ireland. They are a danger to a municipal probity.

But you hear an extraordinary sentence about them throughout Ireland too: everyone says, 'They're people who went on the road at the time of the Famine, and never came in again.'

The Famine is central in the Irish imagination. Rightly or wrongly, it holds a place in the Irish imagination as the ultimate proof of Anglo-Saxon malice. It is to the souls of the Irish what the Holocaust is to the Jews. As the Holocaust is a powerful justification for the politics of Zionism, the Famine has been a powerful spur to the politics of the Irish everywhere in the world. How often was it invoked in the Labour Leagues of Australia or in the corridors of Tammany. Nothing, not even massacre, has the effect on the folk memory that famine does. Here is a rendering, as true as I can make it, of a sighting of famished people in Eritrea in the Horn of Africa in 1987:

> We were led into a long tent supported by hewn logs. Here some thirty women lay on camp cots. They wore dusty but colourful sheets of cloth. Their most prominent feature was the mouth – all the rest of their flesh seemed to have been sucked down towards their eye sockets. Their elbows were prominent too where the cloth exposed them, their arms were each a tendon and a bone barely held in a filament of flesh. Muselmenschen they'd called these figures in the Holocaust. Muslims. These women were literal Muslims. Farmers' wives from the south. Some shared their beds with children, half-naked, aged children, an awful submission in their eyes. There was on each bed room to spare for the scrap of woman, her apostrophe of an infant. Sometimes a child would languidly search in a fold

of cloth for a breast, but finding none would not complain.

The memory of the famines of the Horn will last into the twenty-second century, just as the memory of the Great Hunger is incarnated along Irish roads in the late twentieth century by the presence of the tinkers.

In attempting to understand the enduring influence of the Irish Famine, I think of another tale of the trauma of hunger. I know some women who are survivors of Auschwitz, not of the slave labour section called Monowitz, but of the actual death camp, Auschwitz-Birkenau. That was the apogee of four or five years of hunger which these women had suffered when they arrived there in the fall of 1944.

Now one of these women, a grandmother in Sydney, told me that she never went in to shop in town without taking with her, concealed in her handbag, a crust of bread. Not a pistol, though her gut told her the men with the trucks could appear at any second. But a crust of bread. And so I was walking down Rodeo Drive in Beverly Hills with an American woman who had been in the camp with the grandmother from Sydney. And I mentioned the Sydney grandmother's curious compulsion to carry bread, and there between the Beverly Wilshire and the Brown Derby, the American woman opened her purse, and took her secret out. The rind of bread. The memory of hunger is worse, you would conclude, than the memory of terror. So surely it's obvious, for all their dangerous enchantment, the gypsies cling to the road as those *Unterfrauen* cling to their crusts in Beverly Hills.

*

Now the tinkers live in motor caravans and motor homes. The organiser of an international motorbike rally in Cork expressed his dismay on RTE (Radio Telefís Éireann, the Irish state broadcasting service) at finding that the access route to the track was lined with gypsy encampments. The raggle-taggle gypsy oh! At any one time their encampments have a goodly number of trailers which seem abandoned, as if – within the journey – the people who own them have gone on further travel still. Electric cables are strung at tinker convenience from the main lines across the road to the caravans, indifferent to the question of what international biker's tall motorised workshop may be coming along the road.

People on the road. The aid organisations in the Horn of Africa take it as axiomatic that once the peasants of Tigre or Wolla provinces have taken to the road, it's too late, the disaster has happened.

A number of historians have written about the disaster which sent the Irish on the road in the 1840s. Of the eight million Irish at the end of the summer of 1845, it is believed that up to three million were totally dependent on the potato. Three years in a row, a fungus called *phytophtora infestans* struck the potato, the staple of the rural poor. A powerful regard for market forces inhibited the Home Government, either that of Peel or that of John Russell, from doing much in the way of food supply. There was a powerful terror, the historians say, that handouts of corn would affect the market. These days, aid organisations and Western governments are generous, but the local government wrecks the possibilities of aid through pursuing either preposterous, doctrinaire economic policies, or bankrupting wars, or both. No such complications existed in Ireland in 1845–6. Oxfam, Médecins Sans Frontières, Swiss Red Cross would have possibly greatly reduced the death toll, had they existed. As it was, soup kitchens, relief work and poorhouses made some difference, though Westminster kept reversing its policies under the belief the Irish were working the system.

Many have read and been informed by Cecil Woodham

Smith's famed *The Great Hunger*. The fascinating and accessible historian Robert Kee takes a curious line when talking about the Famine, though. He is always alarmed at the power of Irish mythology, at the idea above all, still harboured amongst the Irish, that the Famine was an arm of policy and not an accident. He wishes to temper the them-and-us picture of the Famine. Curiously he argues that three factors should be kept in mind when looking at the Famine; three stabilising ideas should be taken on board: first, that the Irish were a mixture of many races including the English. Secondly, that those who ruled the Irish were a mixture of many races including Irish. And thirdly, that 'the two populations – British and Irish – had for so long been not only partly racially connected, but also connected politically and administratively that, for all their many differences in characteristics, they could not, then, easily be thought of as belonging to "separate" countries.'

Yet one cannot help asking that if the fraternity was as close as that, why were the infrastructures of Ireland so impoverished; why for instance there were so few corn chandleries to handle the supplies of corn in any case, even if British economic policy had permitted its distribution.

Though the Famine might not have been anywhere near official policy, the questions which lie behind every famine, from Stalin's in the Ukraine in the 1930s, to Haile Selassie's in the mid-1970s and crazy Mengistu's in the 1980s, still remain here: to what extent was it an act of politics, and to what extent was it an act of God? It is characteristic of all famines that people look for their explanation in terms of trials sent by the Deity – a crop fungus or a drought – without asking why systems have to be so run down in a given country that a shift of climate or a failed crop produces disaster for millions.

The question of whether and to what extent the Famine was a willed attempt at genocide still – rightly or wrongly – teases the Irish mind. And the tinkers are part of the fallout.

Given that they are the final victims of the Famine, however, they affect a certain jauntiness.

There it is, night-time television in Ireland. Veteran broadcaster Gay Byrne, the late-night television chat-show host on Fridays, is interviewing first Fay Weldon and then Maeve Binchy, a gentler Maeve than the Ulster goddess whose grave stands like a stone nipple atop the Ox mountains; and then next on is the great Irish soccer hero, sadly blunted, self-declared alcoholic, a laughing boy and tinker-charmer, Georgie Best. Everything okay so far – Ireland's television not to be distinguished from that of the rest of the world – Fay and Maeve and Georgie the characteristic provender of talk shows. But then a man named Dan Rooney appears, and his reason for being on RTE is that he wishes to claim his just rights to the bare-knuckle championship of Ireland, a title which is more than a title, which authorises him to accept the appellation 'King of the Tinkers'. His complaint is that the press has been duped by another tinker into throwing doubt on his succession.

For similar reasons, seventeenth-century William, Prince of Orange, and James, King of England, fought their way across Ireland. Rooney had a video to prove the validity of his claim. It showed the bare-knuckle fight he had fought against the up-till-now presumptive King, Dennis McGinley.

There followed, on every switched-on TV set in Ireland, some extraordinary footage of a bare-knuckle fight in the market square of the northern border town of Crossmaglen in County Armagh. Both the fighters, McGinley and Rooney, were stripped to the waist, and carrying a little royal fat above the kidneys. But their encounter, as depicted here, was savage and willing. They were watched by a crowd of what may have been hundreds but which seemed thousands. The crowd were the movable borders of the fight as it raged its way across the market square. Where the constabulary were –

in this case the abominated Royal Ulster Constabulary – was anyone's guess.

At the point where Rooney claimed to have won the fight, hundreds of McGinley's supporters attacked the Rooney party, and the entire market square was then engaged in battle, Southern tinkers against Northern, with one brave tinker cinematographer keeping shaky record of all that passed.

The tape which was seen on the Gay Byrne Show was a short segment of a long film – seventy-five minutes – on sale throughout the Republic and in the North, crudely shot with a hand-held camera but of powerful impact. On the Gay Byrne Show, Rooney and his handler, a wiry, wry little jockey of a man, sharper than a kidney punch, appealed to Ireland through this new medium, television, for equity in the matter.

Someone in Dublin, a certain Tim Magennis who works for Bord Fáilte (The Irish Tourist Board), a man who loves the oddity and particularity of his nation, had passed me a press clipping in which McGinley had appealed to journalists, telling them that he – as King of the Tinkers – was putting up a pot of 100,000 punts for any member of a travelling clan who would take the title from him in a fist fight at the Ballinasloe Horse Fair. But Rooney's complaint on television was that he did not see why he should have to fight the fight again, since he believed he had McGinley beaten in Crossmaglen. He had been carried shoulder high through the streets as the victor, and as he told Gay Byrne, a local committee had been planning to give him a civic reception to mark his victory, when suddenly this insidious McGinley press release cast doubt on his primacy. What McGinley told the *Irish Press* was, 'The Northerner won't stand a chance . . . and we'll show him who the real champ is.'

For the sake of McGinley and Rooney, I made my way to Ballinasloe for the ancient Horse Fair. Here it is said Napoleon's buyers came to equip his cavalry. There is a legend that even

Marengo, Napoleon's horse, stuffed now and an exhibit in the Musée de l'Armée at the Invalides in Paris, was bought by French purchasing officers at Ballinasloe.

What I think is admirable, or extraordinarily strange about the Horse Fair, is the tradition of the 'tangler'. The tangler enters the transaction once the prospective buyer has wandered off shaking his head. The tangler follows this person. *Sure, I can make the seller see reason.* One or both parties will pay him when the deal is struck.

But more profound still, more subterraneously concerned with subverting the gods, is the tradition of the seller spitting on his own hand and then passing over 'luck money', in that hand, to the buyer. Tim Magennis tells the story of an Arab family, the Maktoums, buying a yearling at a thoroughbred sale. Sheik Maktoum had returned to his seat when he was approached by an Irishman with a spit-smeared hand, one of the essential, magical requirements for someone selling a horse.

'Are you the man who bought my yearling?'

'What yearling?'

'Number 109.'

The sheikh consulted his catalogue. 'I am the man.'

'Well, right you are then.'

And the vendor took his hand and dumped a spit-soggy ten-punt note in it.

Ballinasloe is in east Galway, the area my wife's great-grandfather the convict came from. It is not at all like the western sector, Connemara. This is – to use Yeats's wonderful term – a more 'accustomed, ceremonious' sort of country, and wonderful agriculturally. The towns of this part of Ireland, Roscommon and east Galway, are well laid out. The streets are broader than they are further west in *poitín* territory, and there is always a vast market square, large enough to play football in. I've seen such market squares full of livestock. I've even

71

seen them full of horses and of dark-browed men haggling and considering and looking at fetlocks. To see this is to understand that you are encountering an ageless Irish ceremony. Horse flesh, its trading, the palaver which has always surrounded it.

The Fair at Ballinasloe lasts a week. They sell jumpers one day, flat racers another, hunters another, point-to-point another. They have an entire day for ponies.

I wandered round what turned out to be the tail end of the Fair, and then went to a pub in the high street to enquire whether the showdown had occurred between McGinley and Rooney – or McGinley and whomsoever for that matter.

The barman and the drinkers at the bar told me that it was all blather. The Gardaí would never permit it. Nonetheless, they told me, the tape of the Crossmaglen fight, in its full uncut bloodiness and wobbliness, was still for sale in all the video shops in Ballinasloe.

There was a man at the bar who had bought one of them and therefore had authority. 'Sure it was a cheat,' he told me. 'See, it begins with a four-minute preliminary to the Rooney-McGinley fight. And this is a very bad, brutal fight between two men. One chases the other out amongst the cars. And it ends then with your man fallen there in the carpark, and the other throwing his boot into him every time he raises his head. Now people see this and think that the rest of the tape is going to be that way. But the rest of it is nothing as good as that. The rest of it is an utter disappointment.'

And so we still don't know who the King of the Tinkers is. Did McGinley flee from Rooney, or the other way? Is North or South supreme? It will never be settled by anything as bloody and as harrowing as the Boyne.

It will never be settled at all, except in certain pontifical tinker minds.

# SEVEN

Out in the west of Mayo are the Curraun, Achill Island, and the Curraun Peninsula. This is magnificent country. They take people to Moher in buses only because it is closer to Shannon. But this is the terrible and glorious country. On the Curraun, great platforms of stone slope down to an unappeased Atlantic. A plaque reads, 'A ship of the Levantine squadron of the Spanish Armada, the *San Nicolas Prodaneli*, eight hundred and thirty-four tonnes, twenty-six guns, three hundred and fifty-five men, commanded by Captain Martin Prodanelic,' (which sounds like a Croatian name) 'was wrecked on the shore at Torglass, Curraun Peninsula, on 16th September, 1588. It is believed that only sixteen members of the ship's company survived the wreck.'

From Coleraine to Dingle the ships lie. The names that are known are *Duquesa Santa Anna*, *Juliana*, *Santa Maria del la Vision*, *Larata and Coronada*, *Falco Blanco*, *Mediano*, and *Concepcion del Cino*. All along the West Coast you will see signs to them, and some of the wreckage has been retrieved on the Sligo coast. But I never saw a more terrible place to be shipwrecked than Torglass. It is a heath- and rock-strewn promontory, and one could barely want to imagine what it was like to swim ashore from such a wreck and to find – what did they find? According to some, they found open arms. According to others, massacres. Those who climbed ashore here had already survived the sea battles in the English

73

Channel, and the unpleasantness of having to return home through autumn gales around the north of Scotland and then down the west coast of Ireland. I wonder if they got kindly treatment on the Curraun?

There is a great deal of mythology about the impact of these Armada sailors and soldiers upon the Irish. It's not taken into account that the Spanish traded a great deal with Galway in any case – *vide* Spanish Arch, opposite the Claddagh, in the port of Galway.

In America and Australia, if a family of Irish derivation has olive skin, people knowingly say, 'It's the Armada.' If there's any truth to that, then the Armada survivors must have quickly been soothed by the women of the West.

So was there love or massacre, or was there both?

Massive Achill Island is connected to Curraun by a bridge. It is traditionally part of the *Gaeltacht*, and its economy was and – they say – still is based utterly on money posted back to Achill by emigrants. It has wonderful beaches where the Irish come in summer, but since I can have beaches in Australia, I was pleased I went there in autumn, when the island was grand and desolate, and the light so variable.

Achill is dominated by a mountain called Slievemore, only two thousand or so feet high, but taller than Everest in its ambience, in the authority of its great quartzite face. In a bay on the south side is Kildownet Castle, where Grace O'Malley had a tower. Perhaps between this and her fortress on Inishbofin, she straddled the coast. An old church stands beside it – it may have been built by Grace – and it derived its name from St Dymphne, who fled out here in the ninth century, looking for an inlet safe from Viking raids. Her name is supposed to provide the Downet part of Kildownet.

But what is most startling about Achill, more peculiar even than the Burren, even more arresting, is its neolithic remains, its dolmens and circlets of stones and chamber tombs and prehistoric farms.

And then at Croghaun, a village which they call a *buaile*, a town occupied only in the summer each year, where the side of Slievemore ought to be, there is suddenly an enormity of air. Something has sliced two-fifths of the mountain away. There is an enormous fall into the Atlantic which, at this season, is deep green and turbulent. Here, the authority Achill is able to exercise over the mind is terrible. Lonely and reverent on a bike, intimidated by the gale, I crept in first gear down Slievemore towards these terrible, glorious cliffs, which compete with cliffs at Slieve League in Donegal for the title of Highest in Europe.

I had been in similar weather along the tracks on top of the Cliffs of Moher, but they are homely by comparison with this. Everything here is on such a scale that you wonder how people can live with any sort of confidence in those farmhouses which run up to the cliff edge, and what sort of bovine courage brings those cattle up to the lip of the two-thousand-foot precipice to crop the salty grass.

The cattle are still up there in winter, but many natives of Achill find this side of the island untenable; for the usual Irish reasons: climate and unemployment.

Achill expresses so much about the Irish dilemmas. Even about the stubbornness of the natives. A progressive nineteenth-century Church of Ireland missionary, the Reverend Nangle, founded a Missionary Settlement high up on the southwest flanks of Slievemore, with the purpose of both proselytising the supremely poor Islanders, but also of introducing them to progressive social and agricultural ideas. But it was an utter failure, of the kind which raises the proposition that perhaps people would prefer to retain their poverty if it is inherent to their image of themselves.

Achill therefore poses the Irish question, the one which still bemuses the Irish even in the face of their coming unity with some of the slick Europeans of the EC: can you lose your soul through success? In few countries does the suspicion that you might, prevail so widely in daily life.

*

I arrived at Mount Falcon Castle near Ballina, in County Mayo one grim afternoon, and the nineteenth-century, assertively baronial bulk of the place, the slates and granite of it, were answered by a slaty, granity sky. I sat for a while after switching the engine off, prepared for a cold night in a cold house.

Mount Falcon was one of those Garrison houses-cum-hotels in which I had been kindly offered accommodation. Some of them were brisk Georgian places with conservatories. You approached them with a sense of homecoming. I have said something of these remarkable houses already, and will say more. But Mount Falcon Castle seemed less prepossessing than most. It had an entrance hall built to intimidate – heavy-panelled, multi-portraited, specialising in stern visages.

You can tell by the way I'm cranking up the atmosphere that I am about to tell you that I found, by contrast, the house was run by human beings of extraordinary warmth and vivacity. And that is in fact the case. In the case of Mount Falcon: a singular human of singular warmth and vivacity.

The land-owning family in this region were the Knoxes, and they built Mount Falcon in a period when their class exercised extraordinary security of tenure in the Irish countryside – after the Famine, and after the failure of the Young Ireland rebels in 1848.

In 1930, the English heir of the Knoxes decided he didn't want to occupy the place, despite its closeness to the River Moy and prolific salmon.

He sold it to a Colonel Aldridge and Aldridge's 'child' bride, Constance. The Aldridges were justifiably nervous about

76

buying into Mayo. In 1930, says Constance, the bitter times of the Civil War and of the preceding Troubles were still a living and influential memory. The Aldridges were not taking over Mount Falcon on the terms which had prevailed for the previous eight hundred years. They brought institutionalised authority with them.

Mount Falcon Castle has been Constance Aldridge's home for sixty years now. For the last fifteen of these, she has been widowed, and she claimed that it was not till then that her education in the country home/hotel business began. Now, an octogenarian, she runs the place authoritatively, her chin raised and her lips pressed forward, issuing her welcomes and her commands in a town-and-country accent. Attending to detail in a manner which makes the guest unaware that she has done it.

Mount Falcon is an informal household. The bar runs on an honour system. All the guests dine at the one long table, since Constance prizes conversation and the chance to answer questions about the house and the surrounding country.

You look at her and see in the one person the extent to which the English domiciled in Ireland are subsumed by the Irish themselves. The house can clearly be run only on the basis of the loyalties of the local men and women who work there. Constance's daughter has married an Irish farmer, and I met her tall, slender, polite grandson, who is a star in the local Gaelic football team and who conversed quietly about Gaelic football and Australian football, which are believed to be related to each other.

Her husband, too, was in a way seduced and absorbed by the region. He was attracted there in the first place by the salmon fishing, but then, with a friend who was a local vicar, he began to search out local neolithic tombs and the remnants of neolithic settlements, all in an area which has produced traces of the oldest-yet-found Stone Age farming community.

'He ended up being more involved with the tombs than with the fishing,' said Constance in that slightly surprised, throaty manner the English use to announce all life's major shifts. She had not changed in that regard.

Meanwhile the guests came for the salmon fishing in the summer, and in the winter European woodcock shooters turned up, coming to Ireland because the woodcock of southern France were shot out. Constance comes of hunting-shooting-and-fishing background, from a West Country military family. Therefore she does not seem to believe in conservation as an abstract, but more as a means of ensuring the survival of species for the sake of future admirers, who include huntsmen. But she causes her European shooters to take their sport under the supervision of the local rifle clubs. 'Some of them do blaze away, you know.'

She told me a fascinating thing: the fishermen arrive on St Patrick's day, March 17th, when the salmon run begins. Obviously the saint was given as his own a day of ancient Irish significance, a day to do with the potent turning of the season.

I found at Mount Falcon Castle an American novelist of some renown, Lois Gould. She had come to Mount Falcon for a brief visit eighteen months earlier – it was during a time when she was looking for a cottage to rent and write in somewhere in the surrounding country. In the meantime she stayed at Constance Aldridge's hotel. There was an alcove off the living room of Mount Falcon which Lois – Constance Aldridge said – could use in the afternoons. The afternoons happened to suit Ms Gould's writing programme. The convenience of Mount Falcon's timetable coincided very well with the clock of Lois Gould's talent. And so in the mists, soft rains and deep greens of Mayo, she wrote a book set in blazing Greece. And she stayed on at Mount Falcon.

She grew to love Mayo and wanted to settle and buy a

house. She found amongst the locals a certain nervousness about alienating land to foreigners. This she understands. She says it is based on 'old scars'. The price fluctuates as the natives worry about what the market will stand, and whether the sale should be made in the first place. The stranger is adrift in a sub-text he or she is not competent to interpret.

Lois Gould was not the first human to find the rhythms, the monastic regularity of a guest house, balm to the soul. She went to breakfast with the guests during the breakfast hour, walked the dogs on the great beach at Enniscrone by morning, ran errands for Constance, getting to know the merchants of Ballina thereby, their characters and stratagems. Every night she would dress for dinner and have it with a new group of one-night, two-night, three-night or week-long stayers. Like Constance, she seemed to be proud of the place and enjoy interpreting by answering the same questions. These were the vespers of Mount Falcon. There was a closeness between the older woman and the younger one which an outsider could glibly describe as mother-and-daughter. Glibly, perhaps, but without being too inaccurate.

I was there at an interesting time for the two of them. Lois had finished her book and was wondering whether her own internally-issued licence to remain had been cancelled or not. There was a bath house, crenellated and mock medieval, at the north end of Enniscrone beach. Lois showed it to me. She had made an offer on it. But again the price kept varying. So she began to look at a number of out-of-use coast-guard stations along the north Mayo, south Sligo coast.

She had a loft and a family back in lower Manhattan a block away from where I had lived when I had been teaching at New York University. The simple truth was though that the Irish, for all their ambiguity when it came to real estate and the price of coast-guard stations, had got her in.

One morning I went walking with her and with Constance's

dogs up in Sligo on beautiful Enniscrone beach. Our path was through the sand dunes. She asked me if I had seen the Black Pig in someone's garden on the way here – the statue of the Black Pig of mythology, the one who had swum to Enniscrone fron Donegal, escaping the Ulstermen. It was not adequate for the original Black Pig to be the centre of a number of variant myths. The Black Pig in the person's garden in Enniscrone was itself the basis of variant myths. One of them was that the council of Enniscrone had originally had it sculpted as a civic monument, but had been so ashamed of the result that they had then tried to sell it to members of the public. When members of the public showed no enthusiasm they gave it away to someone. There is a story that it is always turning up in a new person's garden – people carry it through the town at night and dump it as a punishment or a joke. You never know whose garden it will be found in.

The newsagents keep stocks of Black Pig souvenirs, but they hide them under the counter and sell them only to outsiders and on request. The Black Pig is a reproach to Enniscrone's municipal pride.

*

In the sand dunes, sniffed at by Constance's dogs, lives a curious kind of brightly coloured dune snail. Lois Gould collects the shells of the dead ones because they are so perfectly made, but if she gets them home and finds they were only foxing, she brings them back the next day. These are the rituals of her Mount Falcon life. For her and Constance, the castle is Mount Falcon, the strand is Enniscrone, and the holy site is Downpatrick Head – not the more famous one in Down, but the one on the coast of Mayo.

There is still a bath house in operation on the strand of Enniscrone where people can take hot salt water and seaweed baths. The novelist was insistent that I should experience a seaweed bath, but fortunately the seaweed bath house still in modern use was closed up for the winter. I had no chance therefore to ask the man and woman who ran the place what were the benefits of seaweed immersions, and why the Irish set such store in them? Seaweed and kelp were Irish constants. Like peat and emigration.

*

All this on 'Killala's broad bay', where the French landed in 1798, persuaded to it by passionate Wolfe Tone. The landing place is on the west side of the bay in the little fishing port of Kilcummin with its narrow little quay. There are a few monuments to the event, one plaque in French and Gaelic attached to the wall of the small continuous line of terrace houses right on the quay, the other placed there by Maude Gonne MacBride, the Irish Revival's Kathleen ni Houlihan, a hundred years after the landing.

The rising of 1798 seems very simple when you hear it sung about:

> We give you the gallant old West, boys,
>   Where perished our bravest and best.
> When Ireland was bleeding and broken,
>   Hurrah for the men of the West!

The United Irishmen, a largely Belfast-based nationalist organisation joined by that enthusiastic Dublin Protestant, Wolfe Tone, had been savaged by the British authorities. The United Irish leadership fled southwards, planning to link up with the groups of peasant resisters called the Defenders. In the late 1790s, the British authorities were in a dangerous state of panic. The French Admiral Hoche, with Wolfe Tone aboard one of his ships, had already attempted to land an army in Bantry Bay, where only four hundred militia men would have opposed them. But the wind blew fiercely from the east, and the fleet had to give up. Wolfe Tone said that the wind had never blown so fulsomely in England's favour since the Armada.

The aristocratic United Irish Protestant leadership of the day were unable to bring ordinary Protestants with them into the rebellion. For the Orange Lodge had been founded and was absorbing the enthusiasm of the Protestant farmer and tradesman. So, for weight of arms and numbers, the rebel organisation looked to France.

As so often the Dublin administration looked to fierce repression. The Protestant yeomanry, in conjunction with the British regulars, were guilty of unspeakable savageries throughout Ireland, floggings, hangings and half-hangings – repeatedly hanging a man as a form of torture but then letting go of the rope once he lost consciousness. But the militias engaged in the suppression of sedition were often Catholic. As Robert Kee, an enthusiastic commentator on Irish contradictions, wrote, 'The rebels won an important early victory over the North Cork militia in open country at Oulart Hill. Here, incidentally, the difficulty of finding any easy nationalist pattern in the Rebellion is shown by the fact that the Catholic militia were refused mercy by their fellow Catholic captors though they pleaded for it in Irish, a language which Wexford men no longer understood.'

The great battles were, surprisingly, in Wexford and Wicklow, two well-planted and heavily Anglicized counties. A Protestant landlord called Harvey was theoretically in command of what seems to have been a chaotic rebel army. The countryside was traumatised by the savagery of both sides, first by the unrelenting barbarity of the British forces, then by the respondent savagery of the rebels. It was not as simple as that good song, 'Boolavogue'.

I was browsing in a little bookshop in the long main street of Arklow, in country which was severely ravaged in the late 1790s and which had risen in a rebellion of surprising ferocity.

I said to the woman that I was concerned because the guide book I had was a rather straight-laced one (*The Shell Guide*, which tells you accurately where all the dolmens are, but gives you no feel for the fibre of Ireland). It forbore to mention Vinegar Hill. I asked her would the path to Vinegar Hill, the site of the brutal and climactic battle of the 1798 Rebellion, be signposted? I had a special reason, which I will mention later, for wanting to find the place.

She took a step back from the counter, struck a pose, and then in the manner of a convent-school elocution class, the years dropping away from her, she recited:

> At Vinegar Hill, o'er the pleasant Slaney,
> Our gallant heroes stood back to back.

Then she said, 'It's just there by Enniscorthy. You can't miss it.'

If our gallant heroes stood back to back it was because, according to the experts, they had no strategy. They were a rabble, and a brave one, though a minority of them had innocent Protestant blood on their hands.

In any case the idea of United Irishmen and Irishwomen was defeated at Vinegar Hill, and had already been discredited by the atrocities of both sides, atrocities – in good conscience – far more wide-ranging on the British side.

And then, in a far western corner of Ireland, the French intrusion that the rebels of Wexford and Wicklow had been waiting for occurred. Killala's broad bay. Hurrah for the men of the West! Who marched with the French inland. On a country road near Killala, a mere lane too narrow to allow for parking, is a two-thirds life-size statue of a French officer, who may be General Humbert, the leader of the landing force, leaning over a felled boy. The statue honours the first Frenchman to fall on Irish soil in battle. According to what we know, this first casualty would already have been confused by the Irish rebels' enthusiasm for the Virgin and by the degree of resistance the French were meeting in a supposedly oppressed countryside.

The rebels and the French had considerable success at first. They took Killala, marched through Ballina, sent the Red Coats 'flying through old Castlebar. And lo, a voice like thunder spake, the West's awake, the West's awake.'

Then the combined force headed east into Longford. There they found themselves surrounded by two British armies, one of them led by Lord Cornwallis who had earlier been forced to surrender to the Americans at Yorktown.

Wolfe Tone would later attempt to land with French forces in Donegal, but, being captured, would commit suicide with a penknife in his cell in Dublin.

Now, nearly two hundred years later, brave people are still pushing the vision of the United Irishmen and Irishwomen, but it runs up against the same sectarian and historic furies which were in play in Wexford and Wicklow in that terrible summer of '98, and which no doubt rode high through the countryside of Mayo as well.

Vinegar Hill may be precisely located in folk song, but like many Irish landmarks it is not exhaustively signposted. The pilgrim has to do some work. It proves to be a little hill for such prodigious slaughter and such persistent Irish lyricism.

After the '98 Rebellion, a lot of men from Wexford and Wicklow were transported to Australia in a series of ships, the first of which was called *Minerva*. Aboard it, the rebel leaders included General Joseph Holt, who commanded the resistance in Wicklow after Vinegar Hill. He was a Protestant farmer of Roundwood, at the foot of the Wicklow Mountains, and he had joined the rebels after his house at Roundstone was burned down by the militia.

The Irish transportees of the '98 Rising never lost the Wolfe Tone dream – that Napoleon could be persuaded to send French troops to New South Wales, just as he had to Killala. The British authorities in New South Wales attempted to suppress the rebels with horrendous floggings.

Holt was forced to witness the thousand-lash sentence of two *Minerva* convicts called Fitzgerald and Galvin. At last, in 1804, west of Sydney near Parramatta, the convict afterguard of the '98 uprising staged their own Vinegar Hill on a small antipodean tor which – even though there is argument over its exact location, still bears that Wexford name: Vinegar Hill. What sadness there is in that doomed Australian echo of '98. It produced similar results – floggings and hangings, far from the rule of law, ordered by authorities as paranoid of French intrusion as the British in Ireland had been six years earlier.

Some survivors of Vinegar Hill I met their end at Vinegar Hill II. Worth a sad song by somebody.

Holt himself was not involved in the second Vinegar Hill. He had been removed to the ultimate gulag, Norfolk Island, six hundred miles out in the Pacific.

\*

I was therefore under orders from my own history to visit the sites of the Killala landing, but under orders too from the women of Mount Falcon to visit Downpatrick Head. Downpatrick is one of those holy places of St Patrick. A great cliff above an enormous beach. A blowhole, a holy well, this one associated with the cure of a specific illness – throat complaints. (I'd been to one in Donegal which cured warts.) This was a *station* which pilgrims used to visit on the last Sunday in July, Garland Sunday.

Downpatrick is an impressive head, and its abutting beach collects the brunt of the full-throated, fuming Atlantic. Still nothing is more impressive than Croagh Patrick itself. If it is easy to compare mountains to deities, if I've been guilty of doing so figuratively in this account, then Croagh Patrick is the chief diety of Irish geology.

I confess to continuing to rave on about the contrast of the modest elevations of western Ireland's mountains by comparison with their capacity to impose upon the mind. Croagh Patrick is barely more than two and a half thousand feet. It is a cone of quartzite, on which St Patrick fasted during Lent in 441. Over the cliff on the south side of the summit he is said to have cast out all Ireland's serpents and toads, gathering them around him by ringing his bell, and then throwing the bell over the cliff, whence it was retrieved for him by angels. Again, you are tempted to wonder if some Celtic ancestor-hero had been given the credit for ridding Ireland of snakes, and now in legend the merit of that was transferred to the new hero, Patrick.

I have never been to Croagh Patrick on Crom Dubh's Sunday, the last Sunday of July, to go up the mountain with the pilgrims. It is incredible that on these rocky lower slopes, some of the penitents proceed barefooted. The upper stretch, where on the day I climbed it alone I had to turn back because of an un-negotiable mist, is over scree all the way to the summit. It is astounding that so many Irish men and women of average and even less than average health – for the sick come up here too – are able to negotiate this walk which to a passionate hiker would seem an exacting one.

Even at the base of the upper cone, the rituals begin. The pilgrims, saying Hail Marys and Our Fathers, circle St Benignus's monument seven times. These praying laps are called *deiseal*. On the summit the pilgrims kneel and pray, and at the ruins of Teampall Phadraig, St Patrick's Chapel, there are further prayers. Then fifty *deiseal* are performed on a circular path around the summit. At Leaba

Phadraig, Patrick's Bed, prayers are said inside the heap of stones, and then more *deiseal* are made outside it. And so it goes. Is this an old Celtic appeasing-of-stones under another name?

The locals tell you about the penitents who go up on their knees over that lacerating rock. Wearing knee pads, of course. Though some try it without. One is reminded of the parallel *penitentes* of New Mexico, who in Easter Week permit themselves to be flogged with cactus whips, the spines being pulled from their flesh afterwards.

Holy Downpatrick and holy Croagh Patrick are two companion, portentous places on the Mayo coast. It does not serve to dismiss them as examples of Irish superstition or pietism, though in part they are that. It is not sufficient to write them off as folk magic either. The places have a force and dignity that is more than the sum of everything that is done there. The potency of Downpatrick brings Connie and Lois there on a frequent basis, and those women are far removed from pietism or what is referred to as *peasant superstition*.

And what, in a harsh landscape and a hard world, is so evil in peasant superstition, anyhow? In the case of Downpatrick and Croagh Patrick, and in all the other cases, it always chooses to attach itself to places of eminent beauty and pronounced ambience.

Mayo has a more recent holy site: the former village and now miracle boom town of Knock. The Virgin Mary, flanked by St Joseph and St John, appeared on the outer wall of the parish church in 1879. 1879 was a period of acute unhappiness in the West, when bad crops and high rents and evictions were common. This was the year when Michael Davitt of Mayo, a Fenian and nationalist, founded the Land League of Ireland with the purpose of assuaging the hardships of tenant farmers and of those whose only livelihood was to work for tenant farmers. In the same winter (though in a following year) in which the Virgin Mary appeared in Knock, Parnell would annunciate the principles of the boycott. He told the Irish to treat the unjust land agent or landlord in this manner: 'You must show what you think of him on the roadside when you meet him, you must show him in the streets of the town, you must show him at the shop counter . . . even in the house of worship, by leading him into a sort of moral Coventry, by isolating him from the rest of his kind as if he were a leper of old, you must show him your detestation of the crime he has committed.'

These principles would first be put into practice on the shores of Lough Mask against the land agent of Lord Erne, Captain Charles Boycott.

*

Knock has become a shrine equivalent to Lourdes and Fatima, the two other great places of apparition of the late nineteenth and early twentieth century.

The churchmen of the West pushed for an international airport to be built at Knock, to bring in pilgrims from other nations. There are direct flights to and from all the major British airports. Apparently it is not only the devout who travel on these planes. People from London weekending in the West, or fishermen and hunters from England and France, and mere tourists who don't want to have to drive half the length of the long West to reach Mayo, Sligo and Donegal, are also aboard.

Particular imaginations would see an interesting conjunction here along the West Coast – the old sacred sites, Croagh Patrick, Downpatrick, St Patrick's Purgatory in Donegal, and Knock. As St Joseph and St John flanked the Virgin on the wall of Knock church in the same year the Land League was founded, so Croagh Patrick and St

Patrick's Purgatory flank Knock itself. Ireland is the only English-speaking nation in which an international airport would be built for such a reason, and whether that defines Ireland's glory or Ireland's tragedy will always be a matter of argument.

# EIGHT

On three journeys to Ireland, starting from Dublin, and having to visit Cork each time for sentimental reasons, having to travel down to Cobh along those beautiful, verdant lanes which must have created second thoughts in the voluntary emigrants and heartache in the involuntary, I have found it hard to make my way north of Sligo into Donegal. The roads accounted in part for that, and the big farm breakfasts, and the way you have to keep stopping for antiquities and oddities.

I wondered if getting to Donegal would be like the first time I had seen the Cliffs of Moher, or visited plain old Blarney Castle, and other sites much touted by the nostalgic Irish in exile. It was not. Donegal has a most pronounced Irish character, and is sublime in a savage way. It has blasted heaths, and evil, peaty uplands, and exquisite glens and an heroic, high, complicated coastline. All the splendors of Connemara and Achill are compounded here, represented in an even more spacious style.

The county gets its name from the city of Donegal, and the name of the city is derived from the Old Irish for Fort of the Foreigners. Donegal is the Tyrconnel we read about in Gaelic history, and the town of Donegal was headquarters of the leading Gaelic family, the O'Donnells, amongst them the last patriarchs, Red Hugh, who struggled against the Tudors, and Rory, associate of Great Hugh O'Neill of

Tyrone. In 1602 – a long time ago though the results are still visible – both Red Hugh and Rory failed to link up with the Spanish army in Kinsale in Cork and so at last lost their hold. Ultimately, five years later, they would leave Ireland from the beautiful little Lough Swilley port of Rathmullan – the Flight of the Earls the event is still called. Perhaps it is only in tragic Ireland that you can see a road sign with such a portentous message on it: *To the Flight of the Earls.* Standing there in the quiet little port, as if Rory and his chieftain O'Neill themselves needed such indications.

When I was in Rathmullan, posters were already up for a conference of international scholars on the Flight of the Earls, since it is considered germane to what is happening in Ulster now. Robert Kee writes, 'Tyrone was fighting in his own interest for an Irish way of life. It is anachronistic to regard him as fighting for "Ireland" in a modern nationalistic sense.' It is a reasonable enough *caveat.* Nonetheless, when Tyrconnel and Tyrone, the two Earls, left from Lough Swilley on a French ship, forfeiting thereby their lands, they created the conditions for the Plantation of Ulster, and for all its unresolved resentments.

\*

So Donegal is part of the old Kingdom of Ulster. Owing less of its population to the Plantation, the planned settlement of Anglo-Scots in Ulster, than the eastern counties of Ulster did, it was dealt out of the 1922 border-drawing, both to its own delight and to that of the Ulster Loyalists.

Look at the peculiarity of this. The great northern Donegal coast is split into two peninsulas by broad Lough Swilley, as exquisite a waterway as exists in this world. The peninsula to the west is the Fanad, and the one to the east, the Inishowen, culminating in Ireland's northernmost point, the frequently stormy Malin Head. Malin Head was the turning point into the Atlantic proper for many a Belfast emigrant to the United States and Canada. It is part of a sizeable wedge of the South which is more northerly than the North.

So you have to draw a line from Malin Head due south for thirty miles before you come to Muff, on the Northern Ireland border, the home of the playwright Brian Friel, and then further south still you reach the border itself and Derry – or Londonderry – Ulster's second city, on the Foyle.

There must be lots of border-hopping by political activists, and yet Donegal seems so remote from the tormented North. It gives you a sense that most of its griefs are in the past rather than in the present, or else they partake of the traditional Irish griefs: poverty and the drift towards emigration.

For visitors though, Donegal seems to go to a great deal of trouble to be the Ireland of one's expectations. There are, for example, a series of little towns on the Fanad, located in a rough square between Lough Swilley and Mulroy Bay. Ramelton, Rathmullan, Carrowkeel, Millford. As I intimated earlier, all of them harrowed not so much by the Ulster problems twenty miles away, but by unemployment, the threat of emigration hanging over all their young citizens. But in these lovely glens and along this lovely coast, it is hard to remember that. That for ordinary people living in Rathmullan, the nearest employment is in Letterkenny, a meat-and-potatoes town at the mouth of the Lough; that for many, in practice, the nearest certain employment is in Liverpool, London or New York.

Another great house which meets the expectation: Rathmullan House, full of Victorian stained glass and fine nineteenth-century Garrison paintings, and a wide view of Lough Swilley. The concierge is a little jockey of a man called Francy Cooney, barman and factotum, attentive and genial.

My daughter had joined me by then, the same one who had been so concerned about the existence of Peter Pan in the mid-70s but had since moved on to more palpable speculations, like handsome men or a good pint. Francy gave her his card as a joke.

Are we to conclude that Francy's fancy runs free of the problems which begin at the near border? Is he trying to negotiate the bad world with a ready joke. Does the Big Business from Derry impinge?

---

USED CARS  LAND  WHISKEY  MANURE  OATS  FLY SWATTERS
DOUBLE GLAZING  DRY HOLD  SPORTS CARS
MARITAL AIDS BOUGHT AND SOLD
FRANCY COONEY, MAN OF ACTION.
CARS CONVERTED  HOUNDS HUNTED
POKER TAUGHT  REVOLUTIONS STARTED
ASSASSINATIONS PLOTTED  GOVERNMENTS RUN
UPRISINGS QUELLED  CHICKENS PLUCKED
CHANNELS SWUM  STORIES TOLD
GRAIN STORAGE A SPECIALITY  WOMEN SEDUCED
TIGERS TAMED  BARS FILLED
BARS EMPTIED  COMPUTERS VERIFIED
ALLIGATORS CASTRATED  MONEY BORROWED
WINE TASTED  AUTOBIOGRAPHIES SIGNED
BOATS BURNED  INSURANCE-FRAUD A SPECIALITY

---

\*

The road to Glen Columbkille, the Glen of the Donegal saint Columba, is in the spirit of what I have already described. Lovely glens and blasted heaths and sheep on the road. Nice towns trying to sell you Guinness and sweaters and tweed:

Glenties, Ardara. Sheep crowd onto the road, unpanicked by vehicles. Farm dogs, fly to the fact that you can never catch a car the weak way, by pursuing it from behind, take you full on between the headlights. Glengesh Pass is graced, both on its eastern side and on its western, by shrines to the Virgin, and the driver is in need of whatever mercies and percipience the Virgin might bestow. But after a long descent, Glen Columbkille delivers itself, on low ground by a small beach, a bijou *Gaeltacht* village. It survives by its minimalist agriculture, its summer Gaelic school, to which people come from as far away as Tokyo, and its craft co-operative founded by a visionary parish priest, Father McDyer, in the late nineteenth century.

Saint Columba was of the same family as the O'Neills of Tyrone, the family from which Brian Boru came and ultimately Red Hugh the fleeing Earl, which had connections with the west coast of Scotland. He came here in his youth and founded a monastery, as one would expect. His name, like Colmán's, recurs tirelessly around Ireland. But this village is *emphatically* associated with Columbkille.

Right throughout the town and on its outskirts there are a number of stone slabs, marked with crosses, or else there are upright crosses themselves. They mark the fifteen *stations* which Columbkille or Columba followed here both as a penitential route and to redeem the place of its paganism. All the sites are connected with Celtic religion.

There is a Stone Age Celtic ring enclosure which is called St Columbkille's Chapel. A further stone is marked with a cross and is called Columbkille's bed. An old magic well is the seventh station, Columbkille's Well. Screig na nDeamhan is where Columbkille drove out the pagan spirits of the place. A cairn about half a mile from town is called The Place of the Knees. Every June 9th, a *turas* or pilgrimage does a circuit of the *stations*, beginning in the yard of what is now the Church of

Ireland. Columbkille did not only therefore convert Celts. He converted, more importantly, the spirit of the place, giving it a Christian face and therefore compelling the locals to become Christian if they were to have a continuing relationship with their landscape.

Croagh Patrick, so dominant on the Mayo coast, was similarly and earlier converted by Patrick himself, and it hauled with it into the new system of belief every Mayo Celt who had ever seen it on a clear day.

*

This west coast of Donegal is all *Gaeltacht*. It includes the curious little villages called the Rosses, north of Dungloe, spread out on their jumbles of rocky inlet bearing names like Croithli, which happens to be pronounced Crolly.

And if one wants to know just how desolate ground must be before the Irish lost their impulse to farm it, you can answer the question on the wind-stricken, rocky Bloody Foreland, where land hunger took stone fencing all the way along the hard-hearted point to the Atlantic.

And this a monastic place too, of course. Another foundation of Columbkille's; another place to answer Columba's prayer:

> On some island I long to be,
> a rocky promontory looking on
> the coiling surface of the sea.
> To see the shift from ebb tide
> to flood and tell my secret name:
> He who set his back on Ireland.

For though Columbkille would go through his *stations* in Donegal, it was in Iona that he would die.

*

Standing over central Donegal is a granite divinity called Mount Errigal. You creep past it in a desolation which bears a terrible name, the Poisoned Glen. But then at a place called Glenveagh you enter a sweet oasis, in waterfalls and glens abounding, a place in fact where Columbkille is believed to have been born.

I know people from Derryveagh. I knew an Australian priest called Tony Dougherty whose people come from this region. When a friend of mine was making a documentary about the Irish in Australia, entitled piquantly *Echo of a Distant Drum*, he was looking for a sizeable amount to complete the financing of the project. Tony Dougherty came forward and said he could supply the deficit as long as he could make a small speech to camera in Derryveagh, near Gartan Lake in what is now Glenveagh National Park, in front of the place from which his people had been evicted in the atrocious Adair Estate evictions of 1861. Here, two whole communities, either side of the lake, were driven out of their homes and off their tenant farms with a ferocity which would contribute much to the foundation of the Land League.

This foul work was done at the command of an Anglo-Irish landlord whose name still reeks in Donegal – John James Adair. Most of the Derryveagh people emigrated *en masse* to Australia, and in his splendid Donegal vacancy, in the midst of what is now Glenveagh National Park, Adair was able to build the castle of Glenveagh, a particularly splendid nineteenth-century house.

Adair may well have been horrified to find out what happened to his pile. It would eventually be purchased by an Irish American, Henry McIlhenny, who had made a fortune by manufacturing tabasco sauce in Louisiana. In 1983, McIlhenny donated the castle and the gardens to the Irish people.

Meanwhile, the evictions are annually commemorated by a procession in the area, and the memory of the dispossession of the two hundred and forty occupants of Derryveagh is so intense that I have received letters from Donegal asking me to be sure and mention the evictions in this book.

I like the idea of Father Dougherty's revenge. He walked in the procession, he stood by the ruined shore of Gartan Lake, and he made his calm speech to camera. It is exactly as my daughter said to me as we dined in Rathmullan House:

'You only have to wait a generation or two, and sure enough the peasants capture the castle.'

# NINE

Derry partakes of the general schizophrenia of the North. If you look down on it from the great Stone Age fort above the Foyle Valley, the Griannan of Ailleach, you see why the city sits where it is, in its bend of the Foyle. It is older than Dublin. Columbkille, that Donegal lad of prodigious energy, founded a monastery and settlement here in 546, but there had been earlier Celtic settlements. In the last millennium, and under English influence, Doire Columbkille became Derry.

One of the earlier results of the Flight of the Earls from Rathmullan in Donegal, was that Derry and its county were granted to the Twelve Companies of the City of London in 1613. Since then the two names, Derry and *Londonderry*, have been shibboleths. If you utter the word Derry in the Protestant pubs of the Fountain, a Loyalist enclave on the south side of the old city walls, then you will certainly suffer physical assault. In the Catholic pubs of Bogside and Creggan, the utterance of Londonderry will produce the same damage.

The old town of Londonderry has wonderful walls, which in any other place would be considered merely picturesque and remarkably preserved. Picturesque too, at this distance of time, would be the history of the siege of Londonderry in the winter of 1688–9 by King James's forces – the time the Protestant apprentices won their immortality by shutting the Shipquay and Ferryquay Gates against King James's army.

The memory of the siege is the reason for the skeleton which

98

is featured on the city's coat of arms. During it, even the best people in town were reduced to eating rat stew. Eight thousand Protestant citizens perished in its fifteen weeks. Among the survivors was the ten-year-old son of a Protestant clergyman, a child who grew up to be an actor and playwright. George Farquhar.

George makes the old town of Londonderry, and the beautiful Gothic Plantation cathedral of St Columb's, suitable for a mere literary pilgrimage, if it were not for other things. If the siege, that is, wasn't still on.

I was interested in the literary pilgrimage aspects because I knew that Farquhar's play, *The Recruiting Officer*, happened to be the first play ever performed in all the immensity of Australia, in all that slab of wide brown land between the Pacific and the Indian Oceans. That it travelled all that distance with the penal detritus of the British criminal classes, is an indication that Farquhar's plays were the standards of the eighteenth century.

In his work there is no echo of the Londonderry siege. Farquhar would go to Trinity in Dublin, would fall under the spell of Sheridan, whose statue stands outside Trinity today, facing the Bank of Ireland, and would become an habitué of Sheridan's Smock Alley theatre. He is believed to have inflicted a serious injury on a fellow actor in a performance of a play by Dryden, all due to a lack of understanding of the sort of sword he was using. So he went to London and wrote two enormously successful comedies, *The Recruiting Officer* and *The Beaux' Stratagem*. He died at the age of twenty-nine just after *The Beaux' Stratagem* opened at Drury Lane and before its success could deliver him from poverty.

His treatment of sex was sumptuous. He was captious about the character of women as well. If his work reflects in any way the temper of Plantation Derry (even though *The Recruiting*

*Officer* is set in Shrewsbury), then there must have been levity as well as sieges.

But again, the walls of Derry are not simply the walls of the siege and of Farquhar's childhood. They are topped with barbed wire as I write. They are marked with graffiti, Loyalist and Republican. In the southwest corner stands St Columb's cathedral which contains, amongst other treasure, a Jacobite cannonball which was fired into the city with the surrender terms enclosed in it (*No Surrender*, the Loyalist graffiti still shout); and opposite is a fort-within-the-walls. It is a large British Army and RUC fortress, barricaded and equipped with television monitors and high steel-enforced walls, and from the slits in its turrets it looks down upon activities in the Fountain and in Bogside. It looks across too to the western escarpment where solid Victorian villas stand, and to the new suburbs north, and east across the Foyle, to estates which are indistinguishable from those of any solid Midlands town.

Characteristically, few whispers of the Troubles reach these outer, pleasant suburbs; only an occasional echoing detonation from the ghettos beneath the walls. Here in the outer, safer rim of Derry, women go speed walking on the tidy streets, speed walking being – in the season I was in Ireland – the preferred sport of Irishwomen, undertaken in pairs, women striding and throwing out their arms like people who intended to become grandmothers and matriarchs. Women who did not subscribe, except in the more primal areas of their heart perhaps, to the rabid murals of either side. Women of the kind who said, 'I don't know why we can't get more visitors into Ulster, it's so beautiful.' Women who went shopping in the mall below Bishop's Gate and barely noticed – because they were so accustomed to it – the passing patrol, the armoured car with a helmeted, vigilant boy manning the machine gun.

Modern Ulster began here in 1968, when the B-Specials and the Royal Ulster Constabulary attacked a Civil Rights march organised by John Hume and Ivan Cooper, and then carried the war on through the subsequent winter, into the Bogside.

The Civil Rights march had been in protest over inequities in housing, employment, and about the Derry gerrymander by which the Protestant two-fifths of the population were enabled to elect three-fifths of the Londonderry corporation.

The Catholic population lost faith totally in the RUC that winter, as property was destroyed and damage done to human flesh without fear of any legal constraint. The British troops moved in during the summer of 1969, and were at first welcomed as a more neutral arm of 'law and order' than the RUC. But attacks on Nationalists in the Creggan and Bogside were so severe that Prime Minister Jack Lynch of the Republic moved Irish troops to the border and established field hospitals to receive casualties of the Bogside fighting.

With three-fifths of the population of Derry looking for protection, the old IRA stepped into the vacuum. The movement was already showing signs of the tensions which would lead to the eventual split between the Marxist Officials and the traditional, Catholic Provisionals.

One of the sights the soldiers and constabulary members see daily from their fortress within the old walls of Derry is the mural commemorating a new Bloody Sunday. Not the Sunday in 1920 when the Black and Tans opened fire on the crowd in Croke Park, but the Bloody Sunday of the winter of 1972 when thirteen people were shot dead by British paratroopers. In Derry, all bloodshed has its memorial, and every grievance its commemorative mural.

The barbarities of Derry and Belfast led to the British suspending the Northern Parliament at Stormont in 1972 and beginning rule from Westminster. With that came a certain number of civic reforms – the gerrymander of Derry and Belfast was ended. The RUC were for a time disarmed. Carlo Gebler, the son of Edna O'Brien and a writer on these matters, told me in Fermanagh that this disarming of the RUC was a great chance for reconciliation. Yet the Provos, he claims, did not want it to work. After a number of its men had been shot, the RUC was rearmed and returned with a vengeance to their traditional methods of policing.

*

The rich, marshy land of Fermanagh always carried a large native population in spite of all the Plantations. Derry's Nationalist majority derives from the nineteenth and early twentieth centuries, when people flooded in from Donegal and from the Ulster countryside. But the evenly divided population in Fermanagh and Tyrone derives from long-standing native farming and farm-labouring communities. As you would expect, it was the eastern counties, Antrim and Down, and Belfast itself, in which Plantation was most successful. They are all three-quarters Loyalist, Unionist, Protestant.

There would be many civilised folk in all these parts who would want to count themselves out of those labels – Nationalist-Republican; Loyalist-Unionist. There would be people on both sides who took the tag merely as representative of rich personal heritage rather than as a spur to extreme political action.

Nonetheless, the demographics resound; and they do alter as you go west. Beginning with a twenty-six percent of the population of Belfast being Nationalist and therefore Catholic, we finish westward at Londonderry on the Foyle, which is sixty-four percent. Only a fragment of parents send their children to integrated schools. For the rest, schooling, sporting, dancing, drinking can tend to occur in hermetically sealed tribal units. Some brave Ulsterfolk deliberately seek to set up social and institutional surroundings in which integration takes place. But you do not get a sense that the spirit of integration and conciliation sets the Ulster agenda.

In Fermanagh, my daughter and I visited a magnificent Palladian castle near Enniskillen: Castlecoole. Due to an earlier visit by the photographer Paddy Prendergast, we had an introduction, and were asked to lunch by the Earl of Belmore. His ancestor the First Earl built Castlecoole to interior plans by the English architect James Wyatt the junior. Its facade was designed by Richard Johnston, the man who in 1750 built in Dublin, on the site of Trinity's College Green, Daly's Club, touted as the finest gambling house in Europe.

John Belmore is a youngish and very pleasant man whose destiny it is to be the descendant of the First Earl of Belmore, a flamboyant commissioner of tradesmen from all over Europe. Some of the Italian and English artisans who worked on Castlecoole in the 1790s must surely have stayed on and added to the Fermanagh gene pool. And they left the Belmore family with a house of such sumptuous proportions that the young John Belmore must have felt crushed by the prospect of maintaining his inheritance, of keeping it in order, of preventing the damp mists of Lough Erne from eating away at the facade. The National Trust has relieved him of some of the burden. For, along with the great Connolly family Palladian house at Castletown in Kildare, Castlecoole is an Irish wonder.

It is now nearly three hundred and fifty years since the first of this Irish Plantation line bought a spacious parcel of southern Fermanagh land in the seventeenth century. The first Earl himself, who built Castlecoole in the years the rising of 1798 was fermenting, was a member of Grattan's Parliament, and voted against union with England in 1802.

It is fascinating for a proletarian descendant of the Irish, like myself, to find that someone like John Belmore considers himself Irish beyond dispute; that he would not want to see himself as anything but Irish. He tells you how Wyatt designed a gallery around the entrance hall on the supposition that the servants would have their party up there in the gallery while the gentry came and went through the hallway and into the ballroom. This, says Belmore, showed a poor understanding of the Irish, of their ability to hurl bottles over balconies, of the very informal relationship between the two parties to the Irish social contract. So, the first Earl decided that servants would have their knees-up in the basement, rather than in Wyatt's gallery. Wyatt was an Englishman, says Belmore. He never came to Castlecoole to try to connect his abstract design to the realities of Irish society and of the Irish temperament.

The enormity of Castlecoole shows you something of the possibilities Ireland held out for the Plantation landlord. It is now partly open to the public, but there are great wings which have not yet been renovated. In one dehumidified room Wyatt's drawings are stored. In the nursery, for example, there are Victorian and Edwardian toys which would make the V&A's mouth water, and I noticed an eighteenth-century map of Ireland which had been used by governesses long dead to acquaint the young folk of Castlecoole with their geographic situation. Informally, among the rest, are relics of John Belmore's great-grandfather's time in Australia. As Belmore competitively put it, pointing to his handsome wife, 'My great-grandfather was Governor of New South Wales, whereas Mary over there – Mary – her great-uncle was merely Governor of Queensland.' Paintings, Australian claret, ornamental shovels used to turn the first sod for Australian civic developments, ornamental trowels used to lay the first stone on sundry Australian foundations!

There is a suburb of Sydney named Belmore for John Belmore's great-grandfather. Again, the long arm of Fermanagh and Tyrone, the long lines of the Irish connection.

Typically of such great Irish houses, a sort of rural informality is normal. The Irish cattle have come up over the ha-ha and crop the grass right under the Palladian facade. There is a charm to the idea of the castle as farmhouse, and a suspicion that the Irish gentry were eminently set up by the temper of Ireland to accept such irregularities as a matter of course!

I could not help asking myself: what does this aristocratic Irishman think about Fermanagh and the world? What does he think of all Ulster extremism?

\*

Ireland is full of memorials, and they all bespeak the division of the Irish people and the ironies of the Irish situation. The visible memorials of the Republic are all to people who died in the Civil War, in the preceding war against Britain, in the '98, and so on. You have to go into the churches of Ireland to see any reference to the wars in which – in fact – most of the Irishmen who have ever fallen in battle fell: the Crimea, the Boer War, the World Wars, the Falklands. Ireland contributed, for example, as many troops to the British forces in the Great War as Australia did. But their memorials in the Republic are under-the-counter memorials. For example, there is a reference to them in the porch of the Church of Ireland chapel at Drumcliffe, Sligo, beneath Ben Bulben where Yeats lies.

Immediately you cross the border, though, the war memorials, British-style, begin, and the anniversaries of British triumphs and of the sacrifices of Britain's war dead are kept. Here there is no memorial reference to the Member for Fermanagh and South Tyrone, Bobby Sands, who would ultimately die after sixty-five days of hunger in Long Kesh in 1981. But D-Day is remembered, and the Battle of Britain, and all the campaigns to which the Irish, Protestant and Catholic, contributed enormously, some would say disproportionately.

On Remembrance Day 1987 then, a bomb exploded at the Enniskillen War Memorial. According to Carlo Gebler, there was a double action, as with all bombs. First the explosion drove the chain fence of the war memorial forward, crushing the sternums and pelvises of victims. Then, in the vacuum created by this force, a wall behind the crowd fell, burying the maimed. Eleven died and seventy were injured. For Enniskillen people, this was Trouble with a vengeance.

Belmore is a private man, discreet in the expression of opinions – many of those which have inherited the onus of a great pile such as Castlecoole are private men and women. The bombing at Enniskillen has re-affirmed his disapproval of all paramilitary organisations which have flourished through sectarianism and the control they exercise over their own communities. The Earl believes that a united Ireland is an inevitability; but whatever may happen, he sees no home for himself outside Fermanagh.

Places impose their genius on people. America makes people American, Australia makes them Australian, and certainly Ireland makes them Irish. What began as an expedition of convenience in the Plantation became, after a few generations, a matter of self-definition. They tell me that even the English aristocracy feel this way too, rather deriding the Irish aristocracy of which Belmore is a genial and civilised member. Lord Belmore believes that it is time historical divisions were forgotten. He does not deny; he does not pretend everything is sweetness, though he would have some excuse for doing that in quiet Fermanagh, in the wide Belmore acreages. He says that if certain extremist groups had their way, they would have bought the Berlin Wall from the Germans and erected it stone by stone around their paranoid province.

\*

The speed-walking women who say Ulster is beautiful are right. The speed-walking women who say Ulster is vernal and tranquil are nearly right too. Even in the countryside, the fallout from the Troubles is over everything like an impalpable layer of soot. For obviously the countryside and the small town can be randomly dangerous also, though not in any way which should impinge upon the well-being of a traveller.

To the northeast of Derry is a house run by Margaret and Joseph Erwin in the farmlands of Aghadowey, a region so charming and easeful, so close to the Giant's Causeway and to Bushmills historic distillery, the first post-Flight of the Earls licensed still, that you'd think the world should – if there were any equity – want to go there. This house was the parish home of a man who would become Archbishop of Derry, William Alexander – no remarkable fact except that his wife was Cecil Alexander, the woman who wrote 'Once in Royal David's City', 'All Things Bright and Beautiful' and 'There is a Green Hill Far Away'. Her bedroom is to the left at the head of the stairs, with a view of Aghadowey's farmlands and offering a jacuzzi now, a tonic experience Mrs Alexander herself might have found an aid to composition.

Life is peaceful therefore in Aghadowey, and the Erwins' chief worries are to do with horses and horse-floats. Their daughter is a fine equestrian, competes all over Ireland and is a member of the All-Ireland junior team. And Cecil Frances Alexander can seem closer to the true nature of the countryside than the rabidities of Derry could ever be.

*

Here is another instance of how sweet Ulster can be. The coastline of Antrim and County Down is really superb. And on the coast of County Down, in farmland which slopes up to the much-crooned-over mountains of Mourne, stands a lodge called Glassdrumman. It is run by a former Belfast preacher, and is said to be a sort of learning experience for those who work there, who belong to the preacher's commune, which seems a loose and multi-sectarian commune indeed.

Visitors all eat at the one long table, as at Constance Aldridge's, and are taken through two alternative menus by an Englishman in a dinner suit with white gloves. One menu is in the Irish tradition, and is robustly sauced fowl. The other is in the French tradition, and accompanied by less full-throated wines than the ones which go with the Irish. The Englishman, whose name is Barlow, pours Pouilly Fumés and Gewürztraminers, mates the heavy desserts with a Hungarian Takaji or the apple pie with an Australian Muscat Blanc. An extraordinary performance, and if it were occurring anywhere else but within forty-five minutes' drive of Belfast's mean city, people might have to book a year ahead.

No matter how well-ordered the countryside, visitors seem to get a sense of things being weirdly off-key in Ulster. So many travellers say that to you: quietly, not to hurt the feelings of their undeniably wonderful hosts. The truth is that the various parties to the Ulster equation have devised a formula of almost artistic potency, a surrealism probably found only in one other part of the world – Lebanon.

For Ulster is neither peace nor war, and it is both. The travellers you are likely to find there are either the adventurous young of Europe, or people from the Republic who know what the oddity and potential rewards of the place are. People from the Republic certainly seem to like Glassdrumman Lodge.

*

The Giant's Causeway is not far from the Erwins'. It stands in sight of the MacDonnell castle called Dunluce, sitting on a headland, a finer Elsinore than Elsinore itself. It, like the Causeway, has exorbitant tales to it: Sorley Boy MacDonnell furnished it with loot from the Armada ship which ran up on the rocks here. One tempestuous Gaelic night the entire kitchens, cooks and fires, pigs and pans, dogs and maids fell into the sea and vanished. A good primer for the Giant's, which is the most renowned place on the wonderful Ulster coastline between Coleraine and Belfast Lough.

Forbear to yawn off in the face of this statement, for the Giant's Causeway seems a highly significant element in the Ulster mythology. Bushmills, the oldest legal distillery, the hoochery of the Plantation (1608), is hard by the Causeway, so that you go there primed more or less with a free gulp either of Black Bush or of single malt to brace you for the phenomenon.

The Causeway is made of millions of uptilted columnar shafts of basalt, and it does look like someone has begun building a flagged highway which then runs down under the sea. It holds out the promise of a suitable thoroughfare for an Exodus.

It was in the eighteenth and nineteenth centuries that the Causeway became the chief Irish tourist attraction. For Georgian and Victorian folk a journey there was *de rigeur*, part of the essence of the Irish journey. Dublin was essential; the Giant's Causeway was essential. Nothing else was. At that stage, the turbulence of Ireland was less localised in any one of the four kingdoms, Leinster, Munster, Connaught or Ulster. And County Antrim was beautiful, and the natives all spoke Gaelic, as they did in Down also, right up into modern times.

As essential as it was to visit the thing, it was even more necessary to join the debate about whether the trip there was worth the trouble. Doctor Johnson had already set the tone towards the end of the eighteenth century, by giving it a two-cheers review which Boswell recorded: 'Worth seeing, but not worth going to see.' Thackeray didn't approve of it at all: 'Mon Dieu, to think I travelled a hundred and fifty miles to see this.'

But the great nineteenth-century hotel which stands, black and white, above the Causeway is a sign that nobody in the

Victorian era and few since have fully trusted the literary judgement. In the 1880s, a man named Traill built the first electrical tramway in Europe – it was powered by the same River Bush as the water for Bushmills comes from – just to bring in the customers.

Here, in Mr William Traill, we run up against the traditional gift for inventiveness and determination which characterises the Plantation Irish, the Ulstermen and Ulsterwomen. What admirable and energetic folk they are. Of course, their critics would, with some justice, say they weren't performing on a level playing field, with education, political power and commercial opportunity slanted their way. Nonetheless, they – like those other Irish – made enormous contributions to the old world and the new. In Loyalist Belfast they'll complain that people talk about Kennedy being the first Irish-American President. They claim the first three US Presidents to be first-generation Americans (as distinct from the Washingtons, Madisons, Jeffersons who had been Americans for generations) were of Ulster Loyalist descent. I haven't verified this claim, but the timbre of the people make it credible.

The Causeway, composed of its many-sided shafts, runs all the way under the sea to Rathlin Island and on then to the Hebridean islands of Islay, Staffa and Mull, in Scotland.

The Ulster giant of the Giant's Causeway is Finn McCool, chief of the Fianna, a legendary Ulster tribe, and it is variously reported why he built the Causeway. He built it in one version so that he could travel to Scotland to seduce a comely giantess on Staffa. He built it – according to the local interpretation centre at the Causeway – so that he could meet and fight a Caledonian giant-hero who was building a similar thoroughfare from the direction of Fingal's Cave in Mull. Finn, dubious about the proposed encounter, dallied at his end and persuaded his mother to dress him in baby clothes so that she could display him to the Scot and declare, 'This is the child: just imagine the size of the father.' The Caledonian giant, terrified by the suggestion, tore the causeway up as he went retreating across the Irish Sea to Fingal's Cave.

It seems that in this story of deceit, bravado and fear, in the giant who presents himself as an infant, there is a model of Ulster, its spiritual dwarfism, its fear of things the wider world has decided not to fear, the continuity of the province's grief. All changes, but Ulster is locked. In the continuity of its closed camps, Ulster is still the champion. Winston Churchill could in 1922 write in terms which still apply. 'The whole map of Europe has been changed,' wrote Churchill. 'The modes of thought of men, the whole outlook on affairs, the grouping of parties, all have encountered violent and tremendous changes in the deluge of the world. But as the deluge subsides, and the waters fall short, we see the dreary steeples of Fermanagh and Tyrone emerging once again. The integrity of their quarrel is one of the few institutions that has been unaltered in the cataclysm which has swept the world.'

Both sides – the native Irish who swear by their bitter past, and the Orange folk who swear by their besieged one – have beheld each other certainly, but in distorted terms, not as fellow citizens but as a co-existent sub-human race. Like Finn and his Scots equivalent, they are addicted to this distortion. They have torn up the Causeway between them. On that remarkable coast, with its sublime beaches and heroic escarpments, the fable lies geologically wrought.

It lies wrought too in the education *system*, or more correctly systems, of Ulster. Most Ulster children go to the six hundred Protestant-controlled schools or the five-and-a-half hundred Catholic-maintained schools. Slowly some integrated schools have begun – there is one in Enniskillen to which Carlo Gebler sends his children. Twelve exist in all, servicing some two thousand children. In another ten years they expect there'll be another six schools.

All these figures say, are that the two camps are thus separate by choice and intend to be separate by choice in a new century. God forbid that the decree of history should be overturned!

# TEN

So how is it that by comparison with the rest of the English-speaking world the glory and the sadness of the Irish is this historic memory. You would think it might be fading now; now that the Republic and the North both are enthusiastic participants in the new Europe; now that its leaders court Germany, the new superpower, desiring perhaps her dour success; now that the Prime Minister of Ireland takes the cyclical Presidency of the EC and raises visionary matters of environment and the removal of protectionist barriers.

But memory is incarnate in Irish politics, not only in Ulster but in the Republic as well; and in ways you don't find anywhere else in Europe. The political justifications the French draw from the Revolution and the Napoleonic Empire are powerful, but the past is not seen by anyone as providing French politicians with a direct mandate for present policy. The Germans say the past was a mistake committed by other people, not themselves, not their present *tabula rasa* society. Admittedly, they are willing to compensate people beaten up and permanently damaged by SS guards; that is good manners. And you will kindly believe in return please that the SS had nothing to do with us and what we have now.

There are no *tabulae rasae*, no boards wiped clean in Ireland. In any Dublin pub you could still get an argument going on the question of whether the Jacobite (that is, Catholic) cause had already blown its moral credit and its unity before the Battle of the Boyne in 1690. The walls and lamp posts of Belfast and Derry and many an Ulster town are thick with graphic plaques and murals commemorating the Boyne, as if the victory had occurred since the last British Open; and the paving stones of little Presbyterian churches in Antrim and Down were in 1990 painted red, white and blue to honour the living relevance, and cherished and current political significance, of a battle fought three hundred years before.

\*

While I was in Ireland a new biography, *Michael Collins* by Tim Pat Coogan, unleashed a storm of argument in radio, television, the press and the street (for *street*, read perhaps *pub*) about the continuity between the old-style IRA men and the ones who had just recently blown up border control posts, using proxy drivers, on Ulster's southeast and northwest borders.

Michael Collins was the IRA leader who came to terms with the British in Westminster in 1921, terms which allowed for a Free Irish State of twenty-six counties, but also for the creation of a Northern Ireland enclave of six counties which would be ruled from Britain. The Irish Dail (parliament) and the IRA itself split in two over the question of the acceptance of the arrangement. Many IRA forces in the South and West and in the Belfast and Down regions went to war against their own to prevent it. Michael Collins himself was shot dead in August 1922 in Cork supposedly by a diehard Republican sniper, a man who didn't want any counties counted out of the Irish union.

Collins often becomes a hot moral issue in the pages of the *Irish Times,* the *Irish Press* and the *Irish Independent* because, before his death, and while Commander-in-Chief of the Irish forces and an elected member of the Irish parliament, he authorised many assassinations in Ulster and in England. Amongst them was the killing of Sir Henry Wilson, Imperial

Chief of Staff and security advisor to the Loyalist/Unionist Protestants in the North. Wilson was shot down by Collins's operatives outside his home in Eaton Square, Belgravia.

There was a ceremony in Collins's honour while I was in Ireland. It was at his old house at Woodfield near Rosscarbery in Cork, which had been burned down by British forces one day in the spring of 1921. Its burning was directed by one Major Percival of the Essex Regiment who nearly twenty years later would be forced to surrender the burning fortress of Singapore to the Japanese. The Nationalist Irish savour such neatness of event, above all the belief of an eight-hundred-year-colonised people that what goes around comes around.

When Woodfield was restored, leaders of Irish society met there to honour the Big Fellah, as Collins was called, and to explain – or maybe explain away – his connection with present events in the North. The speaker at the ceremony was a former EC Commissioner, Peter Sutherland. Mr Sutherland called up the ghost of Michael, killed too young by a lucky shot at dusk from an IRA sniper, and then declaimed, 'Those who are carrying out vicious and sordid acts of murder and pointless violence in Northern Ireland today must never be allowed to invoke the name or the authority of those who took part in the War of Independence, and least of all of Michael Collins.'

But the argument everywhere is about whether Collins had any more of a mandate for such action than the Provisional IRA has for its own spates of terror. Some subtle Irish argue that the rebels of 1916 – the ones Yeats made holy to the world in his poem 'Easter 1916' – together with Collins at the time he was assassinating British officers in 1920–1, and the Provisional and Regular IRA all equally lack a popular mandate, and are all equally illegitimate.

Conor Cruise O'Brien, former parliamentarian, wrote, 'Some of my colleagues thought of Collins as a paragon of constitutionalism ... But that was them, not him. They, for their part, were shocked by my view of the historical Collins: as a particularly ruthless, crafty, devious, efficient terrorist, and role model for other terrorists. As he was, for example, to the Stern Gang in Israel ... If we really want to take on the Provos – and how many of us do? – we shall have to abolish the cult of Collins, as well as that of Pearse. That does not mean denigrating them as people. It does mean ceasing to hold them forth as role-models for the young. From that, the Provos derive their sense of legitimacy.'

*

People in Ireland debate these historic questions not just to prove their quaintness to the visitor. Ireland is one of those countries that knows history is not a department in some university. It is not something easy for those who aren't good at mathematics. It is life and death. For the Provisional IRA, who amongst other acts of war blew up Harrods; who in 1987 detonated a bomb at a war memorial in Enniskillen, thereby killing a clutch of innocents; who authorised and then bungled the execution of two supposed British soldiers in Holland (in fact, the men turned out to be young Australian lawyers); who blew up Ulster checkpoints using proxy bombers; who put bombs in the London tube – that IRA certainly claims a legitimate continuity from Michael Collins to themselves.

And not only from Michael Collins. At the foot of the Creggan, in the Bogside, the working-class Irish suburb or – as people like to say – *ghetto* of Derry, there is a significant mural. It lists the names of a number of IRA volunteers: 'Vol. Charles England . . . 1985; Vol. Ethyl Lynch . . 1978.' They have all been shot dead by security forces in the past twenty years. Amongst the listed dead are a few who bear my mother's family name: Coyle. The graphic component of the vast wall painting represents a Celtic mist out of which arise two figures – a Gaelic warrior with braided hair, broadsword and buckler, and an IRA man in fatigues, a balaclava, and toting a Kalashnikov. The message of that mural is clear. An interminable history of occupation, of dispossession, gives us our sanction and our purpose.

The moderate majority in the South, Sutherland among them, keep trying to break the nexus, to state it does not exist. For example, a number of Irish politicians pulled out of a planned seventy-fifth anniversary celebration of the Easter uprising of 1916 because the organisers invited Gerry Adams, leader of Sinn Fein, the IRA's political wing. 1916, the message goes, has nothing to do with Ulster at the end of the century. This is not so much a matter of the past being denied. It is a matter of the past being argued to deny the present.

But it is not only on the Nationalist side that history rules, soothes, detains and constricts. Driving up the Shankill Road in the Protestant ghetto of Belfast one evening, I passed under interminable series of red, white and blue pennants, by innumerable murals commemorating the dug-in and determined past of the implanted Ulster folk. Not only mural after mural commemorating the victory of William of Orange over the Irish Catholic forces of his father-in-law James II on the Boyne, a lovely river down south in County Meath. But also murals of the siege of Derry – or in Loyalist parlance Londonderry – in 1688. James II was preparing to send a Catholic regiment called the Redshanks into this then largely Protestant city. Thirteen Presbyterian apprentices solved matters for the dithering city fathers by pushing the gates of the city shut themselves. These days the boys are still pictorially commemorated not only on the brick walls in Londonderry itself, at one end of Ulster, but all up and down the streets off Shankill Road, Belfast, as well. There are also very well-crafted murals of an almost whimsically delineated Edwardian flivver, its interior and running boards full of lean, moustached men bearing rifles:

ULSTER VOLUNTEERS: NO SURRENDER.

On July 12th, when Orangemen march to commemorate the Boyne, they perform a double reference to history, wearing bowler hats in honour of their bowler-hat-wearing great-grandfathers of 1912, who resisted the British government's efforts to incorporate them within a United Ireland then. *Quis separabis?* these tough-minded Unionists, led by Sir Edward Carson and superbly abetted by F.E. Smith, the future Lord Birkenhead, asked Westminster. Who will separate us? The British lacked the resolve to do it. The Unionists in their bowler hats arranged gun-running enterprises to Belfast which went utterly unpunished. The Unionist British Army officers of the Curragh rebelled against the British government and were not court-martialled. The July 12th marchers these days wear their bowler hats in the hope that they can defeat the drift towards a United Ireland as comprehensively as their forebears did in 1912.

Towns along the beautiful coasts of Antrim and Down are bedecked with flags, banners and shields portraying King Billy and speaking of the deliverance from papism and barbarity he represented. 'Kilkeel Still Says No!' declares a banner at the northern entrance to a little coastal town in County Down. What Kilkeel is saying no to is Dublin involvement in its government. This particular negative has now been resonating for seventy-eight years, but that is a modest time by the standards of those engrossed in and hostage to the Irish debate.

If you get lost in the glens of Antrim or beneath the Mourne Mountains, and you must ask for directions, you will always be treated – Orange or Green – with the extremest courtesy. A middle-aged Nationalist beneath the vivid green and yellow murals of Falls Road was so anxious to be sure that my daughter

Shepherding through a Dingle village.

Horse trading at Puck Fair, an ageless Irish ceremony.

Shepherding across a West Mayo beach.

"Savage land, yielding neither water enough to drown a man, nor a tree to hang him, nor soil enough to bury him."
Edmund Ludlow, Cromwell's Lieutenant-General, on the Burren.

Salmon fishing, West Cork.

Riding to the sea: fishing off the Connemara coast.

"What do most of the fellas in Inishbofin do?" I asked the captain of the trawler-ferry. And he replied, "Fook all."

Missionary nuns on Croagh Patrick.

A roadside shrine.

Irish faces.

West Belfast.

A Loyalist mural.

Bealnablath 1990, a ceremony in honour of Michael Collins.

Tinkers in Dublin.

At the seaside, Bray promenade, Wicklow.

and I could find our way back to the centre of Belfast, that he kept walking beside the car calling genial instructions even when the lights changed and we needed to move on. For it is one of the features of the Irish, implanted or native, that they both value the open hand. Their unutterable tragedy is that they reserve their fierceness only for each other.

So everything is weirdly off-key in Ulster. Ulster is neither peace nor war; is both in its own odd way. Enter the car park of a new shopping complex in Belfast and a polite security guard will check under your bonnet for bombs. Fly to London, and you will pass through airport checkpoints, but then find the processing of passengers to be deft and polite and just as quick as anywhere else. See the parked armoured cars by the steel-gated checkpoint in High Street, beneath the Victorian buildings of Belfast, and the humane wreaths hanging on the high steel fences where RUC men ask you polite questions when you make the wrong turn. See the beefy papier-mâché figures of the beaming butchers outside the meateries, but notice that IRA is written on the elbows of some, UVF on the bare arms of others.

Belfast has the same mix of normality and craziness which characterises Derry. It has its good suburbs, and a wonderful zoo, and if you follow either the Falls or the Shankill Roads you come to beautiful country, as you do if you go through high-Victorian South Belfast, out by Queen's University towards Lisburn. But then you pass, highly visible, Long Kesh prison, where extreme Republicans and Loyalists are kept, where the blanket protest began in the '70s, Republicans refusing to wear prison clothes and 'going on the blanket' to demand the status of political prisoner. The Fenians had historically, even aboard the *Hougoumont*, engaged in similar tactics for similar ends. Here in 1981, Bobby Sands starved himself to death for it over sixty-six days. There were historic precedents for that too.

History bites back. You can't just go touring in Ulster.

119

*

One day I drove into the half rustic, half light-industrial and fairly plain town of Dungannon, old seat of the Gaelic O'Neills but drab these days. And all was normality. The pubs were pouring Smithwicks and Guinness, Jamieson and Bushmills with equal fervour. (Because of Irish history, of course, all the distillers and brewers are Protestants, but Ulster people are non-sectarian about the joyful consumption of fermented products.) But with an off-putting suddenness, I encountered a cross between a patrol and an informal checkpoint. On one side of the road was a railway embankment, on the other a line of standard front-door-on-pavement two-storey houses. The checkpoint here was made up of a British infantry section – you can tell they're a British regiment, one is told, and not the Ulster Defence Regiment, because the Ulster Defence Regiment has a harp on its helmets. The officer looked the car over – I was embarrassed by a boot whose lock had broken and which was always suspiciously ajar for meetings like this. He asked if I had a passport.

There was the aforementioned surrealism in the contrast between his spruce politeness and the behaviour of his infantry squad. They all wore camouflage combat gear and had their faces blackened, a sign they were meant to be there for hours yet. Their backs to the railway embankment, they were sweeping the upper floors of the houses across the way with their M-16s. If they were involved in total conventional war, their demeanour could not have been more alert or their equipment more high-powered. Yet through this scene walked women with babies in strollers, and elderly wives pushing shopping trolleys, and men in caps going to the pub. No one looked at anyone else in a direct way. The two realities did not overlap. The soldiers were not aware of the world of shopping, and neither were the shoppers apparently aware of the soldiers.

But they must carry each other in their respective consciousnesses. Denial may take place, but cannot itself ultimately be denied. The potential snipers were on the roofs opposite the railway, and that was what made the soldiers vigilant and self-absorbed, for they could lose their young lives here.

Here is a core-sample then of the Belfast wars, taken from a particular week when I happened to be in Belfast, and sad because the events I recount will soon be forgotten in the welter of subsequent Belfast events.

My first evening on Shankill Road, beneath the ranting banners, two men were dying or about to die in North Belfast of the history recorded in the murals. A Catholic named Dermot McGuiness ran down from his home to a local off-licence where his wife worked and bought a bottle of Bulgarian white wine, a suitable choice for the impending hour, the dark, overcast, slanting-rainy night. He also bought a packet of peanuts for his five-year-old son. On the way back, three men in a vehicle drew level with him and killed him very quickly with fire from their semi-automatics. They couldn't have hoped for a more symbolic, almost sacramental effect – blood and wine running together into the gutter; a mockery of the hated Mass. They were members of the Ulster Freedom Fighters.

Half an hour later, on the Antrim Road, a young former auxiliary of the Royal Ulster Constabulary named Stephen Craig, waiting for a taxi in a hotel carpark, was shot dead by the same sort of strike unit, this time from the IRA. These killings, coming in the midst of frenetic activity by all the paramilitary organisations of Ulster, did not seem to be any more related to each other than other random shootings. That is, Craig's murder does not seem to have been caused by McGuiness's. The murder of McGuiness was in fact a vengeance killing for the shooting of two RUC dog-handlers by the IRA the Saturday before. Such is the tedium of reprisal in Ulster's great discord!

The UFF, in declaring they had shot Dermot McGuiness, also claimed that he was a member of an IRA splinter group, a fact that was denied by two diametrically opposed bodies: the RUC and by the IRA. The IRA claimed that Stephen Craig, the young man in the carpark on the Antrim Road, was an active member of the RUC, powerfully connected within its structures, some sort of undercover man. Again, this was denied by his family and by the RUC. The truth was that for Craig's and McGuiness's various killers the two of them were simply targets of convenience.

The day after his death McGuiness's widow, unable to emerge from the house, nonetheless had written out on a few sheets of paper a remarkable press statement. 'Last night my husband was shot to death because of his religion, and I am too disconsolate to appear in front of the cameras and talk about it. But within half an hour of his death, another young man was shot close by, again for his religion, and I know the grief that his family feels, and I extend my sympathies to them. I know that we both want the killing to stop.' She pleaded that there should be no retaliation for her husband's death. She wanted to meet Craig's family, since, she said, 'Our tears are all the same. My door is open to all who are interested in reconciliation.'

Later that week, when a young former member of the Ulster Defence Regiment was shot down in the town of Dungannon by the IRA, his grieving parents too pleaded in their statements to the press for no retaliation. Nonetheless, within hours the dead body of a County Down Catholic cab driver was found in his burned-out cab on the edge of town. This was a retaliation not only for the Dungannon killing, but for the murder of a Protestant cab driver who was shot dead as he delivered a patient to the Belfast Hospital! In Ulster the motto is not Kurt Vonnegut's stoical, 'And so it goes.' It's a more deathly and Anglo-Celtic, 'And so it is and ever will be.'

122

*

At the major checkpoints into and out of Ulster, you enter a straitened world of speed bumps, high steel screens either side of the road, tall sandbag blockhouses, and young British and Irish soldiers wearing camouflage gear and helmets and carrying M-16s. At the Derry/Donegal border some weeks ago, my vehicle was inspected by a little jockey of a soldier, a native of Liverpool. This was the enemy, I thought, as depicted in all those Irish songs and in the long, slow-burning and wildly flaring history of Irish nationalism. But of course he was probably Scouse, Liverpool Irish, anyhow.

While he asked me questions and chatted, comrades of his in the blockhouse, behind tinted windows, might have been entering our vehicle number into their computer to see what they came up with. If they did, they would have seen it was a rented car, provided by Bord Fáilte, the Irish Tourist Board. At least I was hoping that was what they saw. At every crossing, however casually the Irish took all this unnatural activity, I was never fully at ease.

I was travelling at that stage with my daughter, and the soldier from Liverpool pretended to think she was a bimbo until she put him right. The note of his apology was very much like the ironic apologies any working-class lad in Britain or Ireland makes. Previous to questioning us, he had spent ten minutes searching through a snack foods truck – its interior, its suspension, under its bonnet. So he was probably ready for a bit of whimsical cheek.

Out of all the crossings I made in and out of Ulster I remember him particularly, because he was the British soldier I had the longest conversation with. For example, we had a bit of a chat about Tranmere Rovers, a third division team from the north of England which a businessman I know, the hamper king of England, Peter Johnston, bought and revived.

It shares the same turf as Everton and Liverpool and yet has managed to survive and prosper.

About five days later, in the small hours, operatives of the Provisional IRA took hostage a family called the Gillespies in their house at Carriagh, on the Ulster side of the border near this Buncrana–Derry checkpoint. They had threatened the husband and father Patsy Gillespie in the past, because he worked in the kitchen at Fort George Army Base. Now they wanted him to drive a van containing a thousand-pound bomb into the checkpoint. They told him that if he didn't, his wife and children would be shot dead. They told him that having driven the van into the checkpoint, he was then to leave it. There would be time for him to get away before they detonated the bomb. In reality, they detonated it by remote control as soon as he drew to a stop inside the metal walls of the checkpoint.

Five soldiers died immediately – they were all from the north of England – Blackpool, Warrington, Runcorn, Liverpool, Whitney. The youngest was nineteen and by an irony was Scouse – his name David Sweeney. They found pieces of Patsy Gillespie, Catholic father, over a hundred yards radius. 'No piece bigger than a man's fist,' a member of the bomb squad said.

If you had asked the Provos about this, they would have said, 'Well, he shouldn't be working for the enemy.' If you asked Patsy, he would have said, 'Well, I've got a family to support.'

This action against the Derry–Buncrana checkpoint was matched by a similar hostage-taking and proxy-bomb-dropping exercise against the Newry checkpoint, beneath the Mountains of Mourne on the main road to Dublin. The sixty-nine-year-old who was forced to drive that bomb was tethered to his seat, but managed to wrestle free before the detonation. A twenty-year-old private soldier from the Royal Irish Rangers was killed, and the structures of the checkpoint – metal sheeting, steel uprights – were blown all over the countryside.

By an irony, reality imitating art, Brian Moore, the Belfast-born novelist, had a month or so before published a novel in which proxy-bombing was the basis of the plot. Not that the bombers had read it. If they had, they wouldn't have done what they did.

With sad predictability, the Unionist parliamentarian Ken Maginnis, spokesman for generations of stultified Loyalist thinking, rushed the television cameras in the wake of these deadly demonstrations to demand that the British government introduce selective internment, the sort of policy which had served the IRA well as a recruiting catalyst in the 1970s. *And so it is and ever will be.*

The two explosions had occurred simultaneously about 4 a.m. But an attempt aimed at a British Army regiment, the Sherwood Foresters, at Omagh in County Tyrone did no damage, as only the detonator went off.

Again, the banality of vengeance: the attacks were acts of revenge for the killing in late September, 1990, of two IRA men, Dessie Grewe and Martin McCaughey, by the trigger-mad SAS (Special Air Service, an elite squad of the British Army). You need a passionate tribal mind to keep track of the sequence of pay-back grievances.

Martin McCaughey's funeral was significant for me, because it was the first funeral of an IRA Volunteer I had ever taken particular note of. It was the normal, highly-charged, tragic, grievous, tribal, arresting affair. McCaughey's coffin was carried by his sisters, beautiful, raw-boned Irish girls. It is not fanciful at all to say that in their faces an ancient, unuttered sorrow and an ancient stamped-down resistance were legible. Men in balaclavas fired a salute over the grave, while the leader of Sinn Fein, Gerry Adams, spoke of 'unfinished business'. Armed security forces watched in a sullen phalanx from within the cemetery's perimeter.

It was in fact very likely that amongst the balaclava-wearers

125

that day were members of the teams who some weeks later would blow the Newry and Derry checkpoints to pieces.

And at least, they would have said, we hit the right people this time.

\*

The militant IRA always considered it to be its work to kill British soldiers. But the use of Patsy Gillespie to deliver a bomb is characteristic of another side of their existence: the control the IRA tries to exercise, and largely succeeds in doing, over its own. Like its opponent, the Ulster Defence Association, in its zone of control, it extracts protection money from all businesses in the Catholic sections of Belfast and Derry, and no doubt in other towns as well. Both organisations, IRA and UDA, exercise a rough, often morally hidebound justice of their own.

At the beginning of my time in Ireland, a boy and a girl who were shot dead by the hair-trigger Paratroop Regiment when they tried to run a road block in West Belfast, were in fact running away because they didn't want the IRA to find out that they were joy-riding again. They had already had their two warnings. The punishment for habitual joy-riding is knee-capping. The miscreant is given a time and place at which the punishment is to be performed. He – or she – is also given money to buy liquor. Then they turn up at the appointed place, and are shot through the back of each knee, below the joint – the IRA members who fulfil this ritual punishment have a crude knowledge of anatomy and don't want to blow out the femur. It is curious that most people keep their knee-capping appointments with the IRA. But the alternative is a death swift as the one poor Patsy Gillespie suffered.

\*

In the wide world, the other face of Ulster extremism is often unfairly associated with Ulster Presbyterians. When you utter the words: Ulster Presbyterian, the image which comes instantly to mind is the bullish face of the Reverend Ian Paisley, leader of the Democratic Unionists. Yet the United Irishmen of 1798 fame were founded by three Belfast Presbyterians, and in Penal Days Presbyterians themselves suffered persecution. But the founding of the Orange Lodge in the 1790s swung many Ulstermen in a sectarian direction, in which the most crucial message of the universe seemed to be, 'No Popery'. In the nineteeth century the rabid Reverend Roaring Hugh Hanna beat the drum loudly for 'No Popery' too. His rhetoric was taken up precisely by the Reverend Paisley. That is a characteristic of Ulster: the sectarian debate is waged in an idiom to do with treachery, Popery, heresy, which a late-seventeenth-century preacher would have no trouble understanding and which has died out everywhere else in the English-speaking world.

The Reverend Paisley has found it expedient and reasonable to visit the Israeli occupied West Bank to look at the electrified fence that has been built to help inhibit Palestinian movement. He would very much like to preserve the benefits of the Boyne by running such a fence from Londonderry to Fermanagh to Tyrone to Armagh, then over the mountains of Mourne to the coast of County Down. For he remembers well, and has frequently invoked, the incident in 1641 in which a hundred Protestants at Portadown in Armagh were hurled off a bridge, drowned and martyred by Catholic rebels. Without a fence, he really seems to believe, such atrocities will occur again!

The literature of Sinn Fein, the political wing of the IRA, and the Falls Road murals extolling the dream of freedom gained by resistance, give Paisley and others of like mind a basis for their paranoia.

The more reasonable Northern Protestants, what you could call moderate Unionists, people who like to describe themselves as 'realists', are more concerned by certain lasting aspects of life in the other twenty-six counties of Ireland, the part known as the Republic, than by Popery in the Paisley sense.

They are nervous in the first place at the fact that Articles 2 and 3 of the Republic of Ireland Constitution declare that Irish sovereignty extends to the six counties of Ulster. They are frightened too by the influence of the Church and of Catholic tradition on the Constitution and politics of the South. In a referendum heavily influenced by the Catholic clergy, the people of the Republic voted in 1986 against a change to the Constitution which would have enabled divorce legislation to be introduced. Contraceptives, which young citizens of the Republic used to bring into Ireland in their shoes, are no longer outlawed and are available in chemist's shops. But the majority Catholic ethos does not encourage them, and there is no hope of their promotion as a dampener on the spread of Aids. Mary Robinson, an Irish presidential candidate who, by being forthright about the robustly suppressed aspirations of Irish women, became the first woman President of Ireland, was belaboured by clergy and politicians for raising the condom question in a magazine article during her campaign. Michael Finlan wrote in the *Irish Times*, 'Only in Ireland can a grave and terrible moral issue be fashioned from something that, in other countries, comes in packets of a dozen by inserting a few bob into a lavatory slot machine.'

The Protestant tradition, however debased it has become in parts of Ulster, is one which sees the human pilgrimage differently from the way the clerical lobby in the Republic sees it. The Protestant tradition honours the individual rather than the collectivised conscience. That is one reason the Republic makes solid Ulster folk nervous. The Constitution of the Republic encourages the collective conscience.

Northern Protestants see too that in the Republic Catholicism is counted as an Irish talisman. The history of religious suppression has always encouraged the South to play fast and loose with its definition of what Irishness is. It does so in a way which must cause discomfort to the one-twentieth of its own population who are Protestant, as well as to Protestants in the North. For when it suits its case, the Republic pretends that Nationalism is the same as Catholicism.

By law, RTE Radio plays the Angelus at six in the morning, noon, and at six in the evening. It is astounding to go to the studios of RTE, to be on a talk show say, slotted in between a man who's written a book about the crash of transatlantic corporations, and a jazzy promoter of a fashion show, and to be told by the announcer, the genial cosmopolite Pat Kenny, that, 'We'll just play a song and get the Angelus and the news over, and then you're on.'

And yet Catholicism is not the same as Nationalism at all. For when it suits them, Southern politicians go off to Bodenstown, County Kildare, to commemorate the anniversary of Wolfe Tone's death. The Angelus, you see, was not Wolfe Tone's devotion. Nor was it the devotion of the hero of 1803, Robert Emmet. Nor was it the devotion of Charles Stewart Parnell, the great and doomed Irish parliamentary leader who, but for his scandalous love of Kitty O'Shea, would have achieved Home Rule for Ireland in the 1880s.

Not to labour the point, the Angelus was not the devotion of the great Yeats either, even though he was a member of the Irish Republican Brotherhood and is so beloved by Irish Nationalists. Neither was it the devotion of Countess Markiewicz, a good Anglo-Irish Protestant girl and Irish rebel who married a Polish nobleman. It was not, nor could it ever have been, the devotion of many of the other writers whom Irish Nationalists now claim as their own, and who appear in the posters of Irish literary giants which are on sale to every impressionable American and English literature student who comes to Ireland. Yeats's cherished Maude Gonne McBride never uttered it, Oscar Wilde and George Bernard Shaw (the latter wrote such crusty and wonderful letters to *The Times* of London in defence of the Irish) never let it cross their lips. The Protestant working-class lad Sean O'Casey heard it only from the mouths of others. It was of course the childhood devotion of James Joyce and of Flann O'Brien. But in their work what scorn they poured on Irish pietism!

It was also the devotion of Padraic Pearse, son of an English sculptor, founder of the model Irish National school in Dublin, Gaelic speaker and poet. In 1916, suffused with dreams of Irish independence and of the blood sacrifice that was necessary to achieve it, Pearse – assisted by his close acquaintance with the Angelus – led the main force of the Irish Volunteers to the Post Office in O'Connell Street and read from its steps that resounding proclamation: 'In the name of God, and of the dead generations from which she receives her old tradition of nationhood, Ireland through us summons her children to her flag and strikes for her freedom.'

So – with some recourse to Catholic piety, though against the directives of the Catholic Church – was initiated the holy beauty of which Yeats speaks in his exquisite poem:

> MacDonagh and MacBride
> And Connolly and Pearse
> Now and in time to be,
> Wherever green is worn,
> Are changed, changed utterly:
> A terrible beauty is born.

It is undeniable that in Ireland's struggle for its independence and dignity, a great number of revolutionaries saw their Catholic observance as crucial to their resistance endeavours.

Thomas Ashe, President of the Irish Republican Brotherhood, was the first of the hunger strikers in 1917. Sean O'Casey, his friend, would write a lament for him, but he himself wrote a poem in prison entitled, 'Let Me Carry Your Cross for Ireland, Lord,' a work which was to be found on devotional cards in many a Catholic Missal (Mass book) of that era and even of this:

> Let me carry Your cross for Ireland, Lord!
> For Ireland weak with tears,
> For the aged man of the clouded brow,
> And the child of the tender years;
> For the empty homes of her golden plain;
> For the hopes of her future too!
> Let us carry Your cross for Ireland, Lord,
> For the cause of Roisin Dubh.

There is a song, made for beery throats, frequently sung in Ireland and the diaspora, concerning young Kevin Barry, medical student, hanged in Mountjoy gaol in 1920 for taking part in a shoot-out with British soldiers. At a specially constructed altar, Barry attended Mass twice in his cell on the morning of his execution, and the prison was ringed by five thousand people reciting the rosary and singing hymns.

When six Volunteers were captured by the 'Tans', Auxiliaries and regular troops, in Cork that year and faced a firing squad, Republican women made an altar outside the barracks wall, directed their rosaries at the muzzle of a British tank which kept guard over them, while hearing the prisoners shot one at a time at fifteen-minute intervals. Mother Dodds, a nun who visited the six in their last hours, stated the crucial perception: the men, she said, were, 'Strong in the conviction that the fight for country was a fight for Faith.' The rosary thus became more than a mere prayer. It was a statement of pride, identity, politics.

Tommy Whelan, an IRA Volunteer, wrote before his execution in Kilmainham, 'I have just told my mother that just as a priest starts a new life at ordination, so on Monday I will start a new

131

life that will last forever.' And on the other side of the gun, Collins's hitman Stapleton wrote, 'I often went in and said a little prayer for the people that we'd shot, afterwards.'

Terence MacSwiney, Lord Mayor of Cork, imprisoned by the British in Brixton, undertook the most famous hunger strike of the Troubles. It brought him to death in seventy-three days and attracted the attention of the world to oppression in Ireland. His hunger strike had been begun to protest against 'unnecessary arrests of political representatives'. But it did not proceed, once again, without theological sanction or intense devotional participation from those in Ireland itself, and those outside the walls of Brixton who waited for malnutrition to finish Cork's bright light. MacSwiney had been horrified by the assassination of his predecessor, Mayor Tomas MacCurtain, and now decided to test the empire with his Gandhian strike. The British, with their persistent capacity to oblige Irish nationalism with exactly the wrong oppressive move, helped him by shifting him from Cork to Brixton, where he received attention from the world's press of the kind he might otherwise not have enjoyed. The theological sanction came to him from many sources, including Melbourne's Doctor Mannix, a man who never defined either Australian or Irish nationalism in terms of passivity before the Crown. 'I do not consider the action of the Lord Mayor that of suicide, and I cannot conceive how any priest could refuse him the Sacraments on that account.'

While I was travelling in Ireland, the *Cork Examiner* marked the seventieth anniversary of MacSwiney's death and referred to him as 'martyred', a term which in Catholic Ireland has a strict theological definition.

Thus, at the height of the bloody struggle for Irish independence, the participants were concerned for the moral code and for keeping their connection to the Sacraments open. Doctor Cahalan, the Bishop of Cork, drafted a bill of excommunication for all those who organised or took part in ambushes or kidnappings in his diocese, whether the operative be a member of the diocese or an outsider. This created great concern amongst the IRA. They had to be reassured by the Chaplain of the Cork Brigade, who informed their consciousness by reference to Canon 2242 of the Canon Law of the Church, which did provide for excommunication for kidnapping, ambushing or killing conducted by an individual, but not by an organisation which saw itself – as the Volunteers did – as proceeding with the authority of the Irish state they believed already to exist. 'These acts performed by the Irish Volunteer [of] the Army of the Republic are not only not sinful but are good and meritorious ... Let the boys keep going to Mass and Confession and Communion as usual. There is no necessity for telling a priest in Confession that you went to Mass on Sunday so there is no necessity to tell him one is in the IRA or that one took part in an ambush or killing etc.'

\*

That said, we run up against the contradiction again: when it suits Irish Nationalists, they claim all these Protestants are apostates, while at the same time letting the dour bells of Irish Catholic devotion resonate over their airwaves. Again Conor Cruise O'Brien has something graphic to say on this: 'Irishness is not primarily a question of birth or blood or language; it is the condition of being involved in the Irish situation, and usually of being mauled by it.' Irish identity is obviously either saying the Angelus *or* being a literary genius *or* having taken part in Irish rebellions.

In Fermanagh, Armagh and Down, the Protestant of good will hearing the Angelus sound on RTE, must wonder how long it will take for the 'others' to acknowledge his inevitable part in the main flow of Irish life.

For the great truth of Ireland is that although the native Irish were misused, although their religion was proscribed, although they were slaughtered and sold into slavery by Cromwell, although they were dispossessed, forbidden to hold rank in the army or attend universities, although they were consistently beaten in great battles, despite everything they have captured Irish nationality and so can move it around according to the convenience of the moment.

And the questions which preoccupy the IRA and the Irish today preoccupied them during the historic Troubles, the old post-Great War set of Troubles. A member of the first Irish cabinet, Cathal Brugha, was very intent on taking the war to England. Not only were warehouses burned down in great number, but so also were the homes of a number of Black and Tans dealing out dirt in Ireland. There does therefore seem to be some evidence of a connection between Michael Collins's style of warfare and the Provisional IRA, at least philosophically.

For the fact is that the Irish people of 1920 *did* believe that every parliamentary and constitutional avenue had been exhausted. Well before 1920, the aesthete Yeats had been won to that view:

> Here's to you, Pearse. Your dream, not mine.
> And yet the thought – for this you fell –
> Turns all life's water into wine.
> I listened to high talk from you,
> Thomas MacDonagh, and it seemed
> The words were idle, but they grew
> To nobleness, by death redeemed.

Yeats's successors are not so sure that every parliamentary, constitutional and structural option has yet been exhausted in the North in the 1990s. The bulk of the citizens of the Republic believe that Collins was fighting a war that any rugged and decent man would fight. There was no constitutional or parliamentary means open to Ireland to achieve her longed-for equity. They do not by any means have that certainty about the IRA in the North today. They are not sure that other and more reasonable means will not work. Therefore, on the Sunday afternoon that listeners to RTE heard Peter Sutherland make his speech at Woodfield, over the ashes of Collins's home and life, they would have agreed with him by the million. They would even have an uneasy suspicion that the extreme factions of the IRA are opposed to the trying out of those avenues.

If British policy in the North is maintained at its present level, then perhaps the British government, like that of Lloyd George, will through its supposed toughness but consistent ill-advised tactics, convince the masses of the Irish again that the sword is the only option. But that does not seem to be a possible outcome. The Irish – like most people who have an unjustified reputation for bloodiness – remain in fact a pacific, history-ridden, conscience-flayed race, and will not too easily agree that there is a need for a Collins of the North so late in this century.

\*

What all this shows is that Ireland – North and South – is complicated. It is only in the working-class suburbs and more narrow-minded towns of Ulster, and in manses like that occupied by the Reverend Paisley, that anyone is able to identify with chilling clarity who the *other*, the enemy is. To the scandalously mistreated Catholic working classes of the North, the enemy can be even a mild Protestant Unionist on the one hand, or else a Catholic who works for the security forces in any way. To the Loyalist fanatic, it is any Paddy, however genial. With this taken into account: that to the rabid Loyalist, Catholic priests are of course the dance partners of Babylon's whore.

Outside these two rigid mindsets, in the broad life of all Ireland, the country is fantastically, baroquely complex, and reality and identity shift continually.

Just the same, it seems false to say that there is no solution in the North. Continual efforts at reconciliation occur, initiated both by organisations and individuals. And the checkpoint bombings referred to earlier were an attempt to destroy the Anglo-Irish talks, which were to begin after breakfast on the morning the two bombs exploded. The talks went ahead, between Britain's Northern Ireland Secretary, Peter Brooke, and the Irish Foreign Minister, Gerry Collins. Advancing by centimetres not towards a settlement, but towards agreeing on an ultimate agenda for talks to lead to a settlement.

\*

In one major sense there is deadlock: if there was a referendum in the North tomorrow, the majority would vote – for a mix of reasons from the tribal to the economic, including considerations to do with the British welfare state – to stay in Britain. But then, the other Irish say, the line was drawn in 1922 to go on producing just this result. Why else was heavily Catholic Donegal, really part of the ancient kingdom of Ulster, happily surrendered to the South, if not for fear it would tip the electoral balance? For Ulster is, to quote the London *Times* Insight team, 'The first and biggest gerrymander.' Internally, particularly in heavily Catholic populations like that of Derry, the gerrymander prevails. But Northern Ireland itself has a selectively drawn border. 'Those counties it enclosed in the new province of Ulster had no point or meaning, except as the largest area that the Protestant tribe could hold against the Catholics ... As such the State itself was an immoral concept.'

For that fake line the young soldiers torn apart in the checkpoints died, as did Patsy Gillespie.

It seems to the visitor, therefore, that the knowledge which everyone harbours or is burdened with, the knowledge which – once expressed – often unjustly identifies the speaker as a radical, is that the British will go in time. Like all artificial borders, this border will go, for good or ill. This knowledge adds a special stridency to life in the North, and a quiet, waiting, tentative confidence in the South.

But the confidence is combined with anxiety as well. There will be severe social and political problems involved in the departure of the British, and there will certainly be an attempt by the gunmen of the Provisional IRA to set the political agenda of the Republic, an attempt most politicians and ordinary people in the Republic do not much look forward to. The culminating irony of Ulster may very likely be that it will be the Irish Army who will come in and defeat the IRA. That was the case, Free State against Republicans, in 1922.

But none of this will happen too soon. Through the Anglo-Irish Agreement of 1985, Westminster – against the wailings of Loyalists – has written the Irish government as a force into a position of potential influence within Ulster itself.

In 1921, when Michael Collins marched the forces of the new nation of Ireland into the Four Courts to take formal military control of the country from the British Army, the British officer commanding said to him, 'You're nine minutes late, Mr Collins.' Collins replied, 'After eight hundred years, you can have your nine minutes.' Though Northern Ireland's last nine minutes are some years and oceans of blood away yet, you can hear the clock running. It would be a superb though unlikely outcome if the process were driven by reconciliation rather than fibrous memory, by humane good sense rather than war and casual murder in the streets.

\*

But despite their long and frequently invoked history, the Irish don't always speak as if they are sure what they are: an ancient nation on the one hand or the EC's youngest country. There is a sense in which they suffer what younger countries have: a colonial cringe. Because of their long colonial history, during which a succession of people have had their way with them – the Vikings, the Normans, and interminably the English – they feel both inferior and superior to the rest of the world, and the needle on the gauge of their self-estimation fluctuates wildly.

Recently in Dublin I went to a literary prize-giving. The *Irish Times* and *Aer Lingus* together provide an enormous international prize – some $75,000. The winner of this prize was A.S. Byatt, an English novelist, a retired academic, and it had happened that earlier in the same week, she won the Booker Prize, Britain's premier literary award. Now she had the joy of coming to Dublin on a Friday night to pick up perhaps not as much prestige as the Booker, but certainly a larger cheque.

At the event the then President of Ireland, Doctor Hillery, gave a curious speech. In a small and insignificant nation, he said (beginning to speak in English after the customary stint of Gaelic with which all Irish civic and cultural events begin), publishing was a tough industry. But the Irish were hopeful of certain developments, and hopeful too of the emergence of good writers. He spoke for a while as if there had been none of the glories – Joyce and the boys and girls of the great Irish Revival. He spoke also as if there'd been no Edna O'Brien, Brian Moore, John McGahern, Molly Keane, Seamus Heaney, John Banville, Brian Friel and so on.

Antonia Byatt was a little abashed by this and she made a speech in which she said she was humbled and delighted to stand in a city which had been characterised, immortalised, made part of everyone's mental geography by such titanic writers.

Emboldened by some pints of exquisite Irish Guinness during and after the event, I argued with some Irish journalists that the Irish should show some bravado about this prize. They should call it the Irish Prize pure and simple, and they should give it as the ultimate accolade, the ultimate gesture of grace from the most eloquent people of the English-speaking world to any poor fiction writer anywhere who happens to write a book eloquent enough to pass as honorary Irish. The answer I got from the absolutely charming boyos of the *Irish Times* was that both *Aer Lingus* and the newspaper wanted their name on the prize in the first place; but basically, could the Irish make it wash? Would the international literary community accept such an act of gusto from the Irish? They weren't sure that it would. Their manner was that of, say, a New Zealand literary journalist clinging to the ghost of Katherine Mansfield and in doubt about her literary heirs.

This uncertainty the Irish disarmingly play both ways, just as they play the aforesaid uncertainty about Irish identity. That they are Europe's youngest sovereign state is invoked when they want to find a justification for their problems. That they sang the best songs before anyone else and taught them to the world, that is invoked when they want to feel jaunty! And there's this too: that through what most of them write, they honour a foreign language.

\*

In Ireland there is always a sense of vanished people, a population excluded by historic forces. There is also a powerful sense of a vanished language. It is a language two thousand years old, and the language in which is written Europe's oldest living literature. The fact that the Irish utter English so consummately is coloured by the fact they utter it in a sort of reproach.

The area where Gaelic is spoken, the *Gaeltacht*, has shrunk to a little pocket in Meath and Waterford, and then the far west – the Beara Peninsula in Cork, the Dingle Peninsula in Kerry, Connemara, Mayo and Donegal. It used to be compulsorily taught in Irish schools, but since its place in the education system did nothing to increase its usage, it was then removed from the Republic's legislated curriculum.

Perhaps by the late nineteenth century and the foundation of the Gaelic League, it had already declined too far in use to be able to resist imperial English. Given its geography, it would have been under some assault from English even if the relationship with the English had always been pleasant.

Now, it is regularly spoken by only fifty thousand people, exclusive of the enthusiastic foreigners from New York and Tokyo who want to learn it and who go to Glencolumbcille in Donegal to stay with families of the *Gaeltacht* and to speak their language. I was surprised to find that even on the Syngean Atlantic islands of Inishbofin and Inishturk the children don't speak Gaelic, though some of the adults have a competence in it.

But Gaelic is like the Angelus – the Irish are not going to let you forget that it was once a proscribed language, and broadly spoken too. Not in the big towns which were founded by the Vikings and then exploited by the English – not perhaps in Dublin or Cork City or Limerick; not in the Anglicised counties of the east. But in the countryside it was predominant until the middle of the nineteenth century, and it always had its own literature. It was spoken in new worlds too: ordinary rebels of the 1798 uprising, men from Wicklow and Wexford transported to Australia, caused Governor King and the authorities of New South Wales great concern because they were communicating with each other in this unknown tongue.

The government of the Republic encourages Gaelic for such cultural and historic reasons. It spends money on it, giving special benefits to families and schools in which it is spoken. For example, if a foreigner of Irish descent wanted to know how his ancestors sounded, he could simply tune in *Radio na Gaeltachta* (the *Gaeltacht*-based, Irish-language radio station) on both the AM and FM band, or else watch the Gaelic news or variety show on Irish television. These enterprises are expensive but necessary. For not only are communications in the old tongue a benefit to the *Gaeltacht* itself, not only was Gaelic a persecuted language, not only was it the language spoken on Tara's Hill in the days of the grand kings of Leinster; but also it was the language taken up by the founders of the Gaelic League in the late nineteenth century.

Somehow it became a language associated with Irish resistance. Padraic Pearse, that adoptive Irishman, founded a famous school called Saint Enda's in Dublin at which the children of the privileged classes of Ireland spoke it. Lady Gregory and la belle Markiewicz and all their push were inflamed by their excursions into the Gaelic myths and into the homes of ordinary Gaelic-speakers, and by the genuine riches and souvenirs they brought back. 'Gaelic is my national language,' complained passionate Yeats, 'but it is not my mother tongue.'

The beloved section of the Garrison, Anglo-Irish enthusiasts like Douglas Hyde, Maude Gonne, W.B. Yeats, Countess Markiewicz, by helping revive Gaelic's legitimacy, earned the right to be called what they always aspired to be called: Irish.

Sadly, the intrusion of Gaelic on daily life can seem gratuitous to the visitor. It doesn't, of course, when Clannad sing in it. But there seems a little too much trying in the labelling of every lavatory either *Fir* or *Mná*, and every litter bin *Bruscar*.

In the *Gaeltacht*, the signposts are exclusively in Gaelic, the public buildings are marked in it, the monuments to the great rebellions and to the Famine are written in it. Many monuments in Dublin and throughout the country also carry Gaelic and English, or even Gaelic on its own. So too those roadside crosses which mark the place where some fighter fell in the long resistance. Gaelic is found too even on such recent monuments as the woman in the midst of a fountain who commemorates Dublin's millennium and whom the Irish call *The Floozie in the Jacuzzi*. In Ireland, even the floozies go honoured in the old tongue.

For not all Gaelic literature is pious. Here is a little of Brian Merriman, 1747–1805, in a translation by Arland Ussher:

> Since Mary the Mother of God did conceive
> Without calling the clergy or begging their leave,
> The love-gotten children are famed as the flower
> Of man's procreation and nature's power;
> For love is a lustier sire than law
> And has made them sound without fault or flaw,
> And better and braver in heart and head
> Than the puny breed of the bridal bed . . .

Even amongst non-Gaelic speakers of course, many Gaelic words have a permanent currency in Irish conversation, and so the triumph of this partial usage is absolute in the Republic. People use without self-consciousness terms like *Fianna Fail* (the political party which grew out of the old Republican movement) and know that it means Warriors of Destiny. Everyone knows who the *Taoiseach* (Tea-shook) is – at the time I write this it is that man of cryptic and Druidic face, embattled Charlie Haughey. *Fine Gael,* the old Free State political grouping, the opposition party while I was in Ireland, means the Tribes of Gael. Everyone knows the *Oireachtas* is the Parliament, consisting of *Dail* and *Seanad*. Everyone knows that the President's residence is *Aras an Uachtarain* in Phoenix Park. Everyone knows that *Bord Fáilte* is the Tourist Board.

Gaelic seems to have little more than a decorative force in the Republic. Yet there is a woman who speaks in it on RTE television, a woman of surpassing beauty, a blonde woman, perhaps a Viking and Gaelic amalgam from some stricken glen of the *Gaeltacht*, and when I hear her speak in it, and most sweetly of all, *laugh* while speaking it, then I get a glimmer of what has been lost in its loss. There is always a supposition on the part of imperial languages to decide that they have won out because of their superior aesthetics, that their triumph has nothing to do with regiments. One is shaken to hear that in the Pitjatjantjara language of Central Australia, a region in which in a good year six inches of precipitation falls, there are three hundred words describing rain. Perhaps Gaelic was as diverse and pliable. Aidan Carl Mathews's poignant poem, 'The Death of Irish', suggests so:

> The tide gone out for good,
> Thirty-one words for seaweed
> Whiten on the foreshore.

# ELEVEN

I gave a lift on the Cork road to a young woman who was on her way to meet her boyfriend in Waterford. She had been waiting outside Ireland's most famous factory – Waterford Glass. Just on the western outskirts of that town, I saw a sign saying, 'To the Edmund Ignatius Rice Chapel.' This rang a number of those ineluctable bells from childhood, and I asked the woman would she mind if I made a little diversion and looked for the place?

I had first heard the name Edmund Ignatius Rice in a humid February classroom in Sydney towards the end of the Second World War. How he had grown up in penal Ireland, in a countryside preyed upon by bounty hunters looking for priests, and how he had hit on his strategem for educating the poor.

But the hillside we drove up looking for traces of him was complicated. It was yet again a case of the Irish giving general rather than specific indications. Pilgrims have to spend a bit of time on enquiries. That's the proper way of the world as the Irish have up to now perceived it.

It meant I couldn't find the chapel, and though my passenger was patient, I decided that I'd better get her to her rendezvous.

I came back to the hill that afternoon. I had spent the day visiting other Waterford glories. Near the quay is a tower attributed to a Dane called Reginaldo. For Waterford is a

Viking city, like all of Ireland's major seaports. As with all Irish seaports too the Vikings were replaced by the Normans, in Waterford's case by the graphically named Strongbow, Earl of Pembroke. One could say Waterford was staunchly English. *Urbs Intacta Manet Waterfordia*, says its motto. *Waterford remains, an unyielding city!* It didn't remain intact from Cromwell, though it made him exercise his forces in two sieges before it yielded.

The tower attributed to Reginaldo and believed to be the oldest tower of mortared stone in all Europe has mementoes of the long occupation – Royal Charters, ceremonial swords of King John and Henry VIII, and a Charter Roll of Richard II.

Waterford has a pleasant waterfront too, though the traffic which comes in over the Edmund Ignatius Rice bridge is heavy enough, trucks making for Cork or northeast to Dublin. Along the front is a hotel where Meagher of the Sword, one of the leaders of Young Ireland, was born. After that abortive affair in 1848, he was transported to Tasmania, escaped to the United States and became a famous Civil War general on the Union side after helping to raise the Fighting 69th of New York and serving as its colonel. He ended his life as Acting Governor of Montana, where his sense of equity towards the Indians provoked vigilantes into drowning him in the Missouri; a long way from the broad and genial Suir on which Waterford stands. Meagher chokes in darkness at last on the fullness of his own life.

So I made my ineffectual mental memorial for Meagher – I'd always liked the stylish way he had escaped from Tasmania, giving his parole and then withdrawing it by dashing in from his horse at Sorrell police station in Tasmania and crying, 'By the way, I'm taking my parole back.' Then to horse, three days hiding with English sympathisers in the bush. Then the whaler, and the Civil War awaiting. A Christian Brother who taught me, an Australian named Jimmy McGlade, aesthete, classic batsman and fine Rugby League coach, writes to me at least once a year asking whether I am ready yet to produce a great work on Meagher of the Sword.

After the waterfront, I returned to where I was staying, the plush Waterford Castle with its strenuous panelling, enormous vivid carpets and criminally fine dining. It is reached by a punt, a ferry, across a reach of the Suir estuary, and in late afternoon I caught the ferry back to town, compelled by Brother Rice's memory. I went through town and then west to Mount Sion, this particular version of it a hill outside Waterford, and looked again for Edmund Ignatius.

Sion is a hill covered with the sort of dour gothic-revival architecture the Irish spread from here all over a suffering globe. When, in late afternoon, I found the Christian Brothers School there, it too looked identical to the one I'd begun to attend in the Western Suburbs of Sydney at the age of eight, the one in which I first heard the term 'Isle of Saints and Scholars', and other indelible tags and aphorisms.

Edmund Ignatius Rice had always seemed a slightly glamour-ous figure by comparison with the often meat-fisted Irishmen and Irish Australians who belonged to his Order. He had attended a hedge school in Callan. He played hurling. The love of sport which characterised the Christian Brothers and the Irish countryside from which they sprung was there in Rice's youth. A pamphlet which the brothers on Mount Sion pub-lished to honour Rice has time to honour an eighteenth-century hurler, Lord Cuff of Desart, in a translation from the Gaelic:

> A sigh comes from many a heart.
> Acid tears fall on many a cheek
> At not beholding thee
> With green jacket and crimson cap
> Leading out the nimble hurlers.

One is reminded again of the bold Thaddy Quill, that

Muskerry champion who attracted to his name an enthusiastic song of praise:

> For ramblin', for rovin',
> For football and courtin',
> And drinking black porter as fast as you fill,
> In all your day's roamin'
> You'll find none more jovial
> Than the Muskerry sportsman the bold Thaddy Quill.

There were some good stories attaching to Brother Rice. In the '98 Rising, a young man called Cahill who would later join Edmund Ignatius in his new Order, was saved by the intervention of a Church of Ireland minister from flaying to death at the hands of the yeomen. One of Rice's brothers was a United Irishman and had to be smuggled out of Waterford in a meat barrel aboard a ship.

Edmund Ignatius had been married too, which few of the brothers who taught us could boast of. He ran a successful business in Waterford and addressed himself to the question of the lost boys of the city. He began a school for them in a stable in New Street, Waterford. Then he moved out to Mount Sion. The education he offered was comprehensive and – for its time – revolutionary. He had a bakery on the premises to feed his pupils, and a number of friendly tailors to set them up with new suits of clothing. In 1809, Edmund Rice and his followers – Grosvenor, Mulcahy, Hogan, Power, and Dunphy – took simple vows and became monks.

A snobbish Jesuit boy, James Joyce, took a similar list of Christian Brother names in *Portrait of the Artist* and poured some scorn upon them:

> A squad of christian brothers was on its way back
> from the Bull and had begun to pass, two by two,
> across the bridge ... The uncouth faces passed

him two by two, stained yellow or red or livid
by the sea . . . he tried to hide his face from their
eyes by gazing down sideways into the shallow
swirling water under the bridge but he still saw
a reflection therein of their topheavy silk hats and
humble tapelike collars and loosely hanging clerical
clothes.

> – Brother Hickey
> Brother Quaid
> Brother MacArdle
> Brother Keogh –

Their piety would be like their faces, like their
clothes; and it was idle for him to tell himself that
their humble and contrite hearts, it might be, paid
a far richer tribute of devotion than his had ever
been . . .

Edmund Ignatius Rice's followers went into places the
Jesuits would never go. In my case they went to the then
western limit of Sydney, to a place called Strathfield, and their
simple ambition was to take us snot-nosed Aussies and inject
us into the mainstream of the Anglo-Saxon professions, while
still ensuring that we kept our holy faith. They succeeded in
the first regard very broadly, but did not always have success
in the second. And their names were names which Ireland's
great writer would have treated with derision: McEligott,
McAppion, Murphy Molloy, O'Connor, McMahon . . .

Edmund Ignatius Rice's remains now lie in a fairly modern cream brick chapel – the equally offensive successor of
neo-gothic – in the grounds of the school he founded. Big
lads with musical instruments in their hands, or idly swinging
hurley sticks, lope past it. Middle-aged remembrancers of
the muscular Christian Brothers' education the world over,

men who thought they'd escaped Edmund Ignatius for good, come here to see the coffin behind its glass screen. Various prayers for the intercession of Edmund Ignatius, and for the Confirmation of his Virtues (with an eye to canonisation) are inset in the railing of the kneeler by the glass. On a sheet you can pick up at the door of the chapel is the plea that any favours received through his intercession should be reported to the nearest Brothers' monastery or to the Brothers at Westcourt, Callan, County Kilkenny. If this were not such a secular age, his chances of canonisation would have been pretty high, but even in Ireland his congregation is dwindling.

So he has to depend on more mundane miracles, the occasional half-bemused arrival of one of his ageing boys from far places. I wonder does he know how strong some of his children are in the Australian Labour Party, and how robust are their political chicaneries, their livers, their sense of embattled clanhood?

For they too are amongst his wonders.

# TWELVE

The Boyne is a favoured valley. The white cow goddess Boand enriched its source by drowning herself there.

By the rich Boyne too, new Stone Age farmers found the leisure and plenty you need for civilised life. The promise of the Boyne is still there, implicit in the rich, broad floodplain. *There is not in this wide world a valley so etc*. The Boyne, enriched by the sacrifices of holy cows, was Fat Valley. This whole region: the Boyne and the Blackwater; bountiful Meath. Here St Patrick chose to light the Paschal Fire at Easter in AD 443, knowing that this was a valley pregnant with Gaelic gods, with Dagda, Boand, Oengus, Grainne, Diarmuid; knowing what he was up against.

The Boyne would give the monks of Kells the leisure to be civilised. Both the old-style Columban monks, and the fancier, reforming twelfth-century Cistercians who came to Ireland to clean things up, chose the area. Mellifont, the founding Cistercian abbey, lies not far north of the line King Billy later took up for his celebrated and tediously invoked attack on the Jacobites. The Boyne enabled the high kings to live on Tara and run a heroically long banqueting hall along the line of that hill smaller than most decent-sized hills anywhere else, but taller than Everest in legend. (The protocols of this gigantic eating area are presented diagrammatically in the *Book of Leinster*.)

I have heard the word Boyne uttered by grandparents in Australia as a venue of loss. I have heard the name of Drogheda,

150

the port town at the mouth of the Boyne estuary. 'Being in the heat of action,' wrote Cromwell, 'I forbade them to spare any that were in arms in the town . . . I am persuaded that this is a righteous judgement of God upon these barbarous wretches . . .' Hence the renowned Cromwellian massacre of the citizens of Drogheda, men, women, children, priests, nuns.

So, I was utterly unprepared for the Boyne's sweetness, charm, beauty, promise and sober magic.

The magic is significant: there are enough symmetrical mounds visible from the air, enough spaceship-shaped chamber tombs keyed to the solstices, to keep a van Daniken primed with supposed connections between the Boyne and the outer, the supranormal, the astral.

The glistening quartzite exterior wall of the great tomb at Newgrange is made of stone which comes from Wicklow, and some of the other stones used come from Cork. Weighing sometimes three or four tons, stones were brought down to the rich Boyne without use of the wheel. All these giant stones, including those cunningly placed to make the roof of the burial chamber, were transported by sledge. The young man who showed us Newgrange said that it had taken labour spread over thirty years to finish the great tomb. He said of the neolithic farmers, 'We know this about them: they *really* wanted to make it.'

Gentlemen antiquarians of the Plantation penetrated the long narrow entry and the burial chamber of Newgrange late in the seventeenth century. They found the dust, waiting on basin-shaped stones in three alcoves, of those Boyne farmers who had possessed sufficient esteem to have their ashes included in this chamber of chambers.

It was not until modern times, 1963, that a peculiar device in the roof of the passage into the tomb was discovered: the roof-box. The edge of the coping stone of this opening is decorated with the same circular design you see on the stones in the burial chamber, and which would be taken up by Celtic artists. The stone roof-box itself is an aperture which exists to admit a ray of light to the burial chamber at daybreak on the shortest day of the year. The entire structure must have been built around this device, or at least around the concept of it.

*

Only the dust and ashes and bone fragments of the neolithic elect were placed here on the great basin stones, and so only the contemporary elect – a few officials from Dublin, Drogheda, Slane and Navan – get tickets to come here every winter solstice, December 21st, and see the chamber fill up with rosy light between two minutes to nine and about twenty after the hour. The only natural light that ever enters the chamber.

What is it about the sun at the solstice? A long way from Meath, on the mesas of Utah and Colorado, the Anasazi Indians built towers with slits designed for no other purpose than to catch the solstice sun at daylight or sunset. Here in Meath, it is Newgrange which captures the winter solstice sunrise.

The Valley of the Boyne device built to look after the solstice sunset is a little downstream, at Dowth, which is said to be a name derived from the Irish *dubad*, darkness. A druid wanted to build a tower here – according to the Boyne's plentiful mythology – and he contracted all the men of Erin for a single day. (The myth itself shows sign that on Tara's hill in Celtic times the phrase 'the men of Erin' was commonly used and that therefore, through their shared language, the Irish had nationality early.) In any case, the druid's sister helped him by putting a spell on the sun, so that it would not sink until the tower was finished. She committed incest with her brother, however, and the sun set. Before going, it filled Dowth's central chamber with its light.

*

The entrance into Dowth too is narrow to the point of claustrophobia.

The passage tombs of Dowth and Knowth and Newgrange, which contribute so much to the ambience of the valley, are meant to represent the fierce passages of life and death. To enter Newgrange you had, in earlier times, to climb over a decorated kerb stone with potent symbols pecked in it by stone instruments; and then the passage in itself was strict and threatening and caused you to stoop.

In the burial chamber, the dead lay all year until liberated at sunrise on the year's most alarming day, the shortest, the one which would not necessarily yield itself up to a turning of the year but which might only be a prelude to shorter and shorter days and then eternal night.

But on that one triumphal blast of light at two minutes to nine in neolithic Ireland, the spirits rose lightly and escaped the narrowly entered bourn of death.

The myth about the druid and his sister is interesting, because there are many similar incest myths in the central deserts of Australia amongst tribal Aboriginals. The myths of Christian Ireland are of a different nature, and they show how uneasy these pagan sites made the Christians. There is a story that Cormac mac Airt, High King of Tara, after whom one of the mounds on Tara is named, told his court that he did not want to be buried at the *Brugh Na Boinne*, the gravesites of the Boyne. They were, he said, burial places for idolaters. The fact that some of his court thought of burying him there in the first place is a tribute to the significance of Newgrange. In any case, after his death, some of his servants decided to take his body there from south of the Boyne. The river 'swelled up thrice, so as that they could not come', and Cormac the Christian was buried on the south side of the Boyne after all.

Of Cormac of Tara, the lovely *Book of Leinster* says:

Since Solomon was,
who was better than all progenies together,
what offspring that would match Cormac
hath the earth devoured, O God?

Ireland is so plump with this sort of tale, Christian and Druidic. Kick a stone and fable goes tumbling. Upstream at Trim, there is an open-air tomb – in the cemetery of Newtown Cathedral – which is called 'The Jealous Man and Woman'. This is the burial place of Sir Lucas Dillon and his wife Lady Jane Bathe. The weathered stone tresses of Lady Jane Bathe's effigy are full of rusty pins. People put them there in thanks for the rain water taken from Lady Jane's stone hair, which is used to cure warts. The pins must be for Lady Jane's toilet. In Ireland of the European Community and the Economic Union, where the heavy trucks pound south from Navan to Trim, still nearly everything means something fantastic. The geologic strata are nothing beside the strata of fable.

In fact, as at Croagh Patrick, frequently the two are the same.

# THIRTEEN

Patrick Kavanagh writes in 1938 (the year of the 'Munich bother') of an argument over a field. He describes a set of males named the Duffys, and then a solitary figure named old McCabe, stamping about and arguing over who owned:

> That half a rood of rock, a no-man's land
> Surrounded by our pitchfork-armed claims.

He says in the poem that he felt a tendency in such important times to discount this argument, until:

> Homer's ghost came whispering to my mind
> He said: I made the Iliad from such
> A local row. Gods make their own importance.

The Irish capacity to exalt themselves to deity status and to give significance to what is – after all – a small moist, fog-bound island at the northwest limit of Europe, is still potent. The Irish invention of Ireland and of themselves may be their greatest act of genius. Their capacity to consecrate and therefore to aggrandise is there in the myth-making, and in their capacity to mythologise Dublin itself and to make it the capital city of the Western world's imagination. All a matter of a rood here and a yard there, of a short stroll from one giant event to the next.

I remember walking with an Irishman along Lower Mount Street and past Merrion Square towards Nassau Street and

Trinity College. Right on the corner of Merrion Square is the Georgian house which once belonged to Oscar Wilde's distinguished father, an author and a surgeon. The young Oscar knew this facade, this corner, this small but piquant Dublin sky, these doorways.

Barely more than the length of a cricket pitch further east, along the line Bloom himself took in *Ulysses*, asking himself questions about Parnell and A.E.; ('A.E.: what does that mean? Initials perhaps . . .') you come to the greengrocer's which used to be the hotel where Nora Barnacle worked. We know the day Joyce fell in love with her – June 16th. Bloomsday itself, a humanist Holiday of Obligation. This was in 1904, all in this small space.

The Irishman I was with took me to the side of the former hotel, where it abutted onto Trinity College, and pointed up through the leaves of a tall tree to the residual paintwork which still says *Finns's Hotel*.

This intimacy of the city of Dublin takes the breath of someone from a vast country where wonders are more sparsely distributed. Along here, Nassau Street, by the railings of Trinity College, such strollers came and went: Wilde and Shaw, Moore, Gogarty, Gonne, Synge, O'Casey, Yeats and Joyce and Beckett; and years before them of course, Congreve, Farquhar, Swift, Burke, Goldsmith and Sheridan. They made this town higher in the European imagination than the Rockies and vaster than the Great Plains.

And yet, looked at objectively, which we never can manage anyhow, and divorced from its glories, the city could be seen as relatively plain in itself. If not for its remnant Georgian architecture, it might perhaps even seem a drab little provincial town. Plainly situated; a narrow and defensible position on an undistinguished estuary. The Liffey not even as large as Melbourne's Yarra or New York's East, and no more inherently suitable to become the Ganges of the literary imagination.

156

Trinity itself an intimate and provincial university with a small but very fine facade facing College Green.

Minute by the standards of Nôtre-Dame or Chapel Hill, it hit it big with its bright boys and girls, and its collection of extraordinary monastic manuscripts.

Again, such a wide street crossing from the front of Trinity to the superb front of the Bank of Ireland, Ireland's parliament from 1729 till it voted itself out of existence in 1802. Grattan's Parliament of which the Irish speak with a kind of respectful yearning. Grattan tried to achieve an Irish Garrison and Ascendancy rebellion against the English, one akin to Washington's and Jefferson's. It looked for a time as if the Anglo-Irish would bite the hand which had placed them in their sweet position. The idea came to ruin with the Act of Union, a parliamentary bill which would cost all parties to it very dearly.

*

Coming to Dublin, I have always wondered why on the signposts its Gaelic name is Ath Cliath. It seems though there were two Celtic settlements in existence when the Vikings made their outpost there: Ath Cliath (Baile Atha Cliath, Town of Hurdles because of a ford over the river) and on the south side Duibhlinn, the Dark Pool, a deep anchorage. Ath Cliath probably wins its place on the signposts since that's the side the Post Office is on.

It is hard to know why the Irish government ordained 1988 as the Dublin millennium, since the first Norse fleet came in 841. Olaf the White established a fortress where Dublin Castle now stands, on the rare hill to the west of then Dublin. Well before 988 there were fights for possession of Dublin between the Norse and the Kings from Tara up in Meath, and the Norse King of Dublin became King of York too in 923, before in 937 the town was burned by Donnchad Donn of Tara. I have guidebooks which do not even mention 988 in the chronology of the city. However I do not know enough to accuse the Irish of seizing the commercial opportunity inherent in a 1988 millennium. And now that the Floozie in the Jacuzzi sits gauntly in the sheets of water of a monument which says 988, we are stuck with the date.

Ath Cliath. Dublin. The piddle of the Liffey between. The Dubliners still argue about the north and south sides of the river, in mimicry of more serious battles elsewhere along similar lines.

This is the catalogue of the northside's wonders. The Post Office. The long, potentially splendid and now sadly tawdry sweep of O'Connell Street, saved from crassness by the facade of the Gresham, by the bullet-pocked statue of O'Connell, by the very satisfying statue of James Larkin in mid-oration, an eloquent passage from Sean O'Casey on its side. The Georgian Customs House eastwards, the Georgian Four Courts to the west; two splendid buildings. The architectural guides say that most of the Georgian building boom was in fact on this side of the river. Decaying Mountjoy Square would support this argument. And the red-bricked Parnell Square near the Gate Theatre.

In the early twentieth and late nineteenth centuries rows of mid-eighteenth-century houses were pulled down to make way for tenements which are themselves now in ruins. They say that at the time of the Post Office Rebellion, Dublin – both sides of the Liffey – had the worst slums in Europe.

Again the northside: the great Phoenix Park, where in the Viceregal Lodge the social seasons of Dublin distracted the Garrison from opinion in the street and the country lane. These days, the Park's great spaces seem as crucial a delight in this city as Central Park is in New York.

Northside are the theatres of greatest renown: the Gate and the Abbey. The suburbs: Dollymount, Clontarf, Howth, all touched by the salt breath of the Irish Sea; respectable

Drumcondra inland, and the suburbs and housing estates on the way to the airport.

The sign of contradiction on this side of the river is the Post Office. The last widely celebrated anniversary of Easter 1916, the fiftieth, in 1966, was marked in a full-throated Republican manner. Vast portraits of the Post Office leaders were hung in Croke Park, songs of revolution were sung, bands played and cannon spewed thunder. But that was two years before the Troubles of the North began; three years before the IRA surfaced again and the Provos were born.

As the seventy-fifth anniversary bore down on this civilised nation late in the century, in the shadow of mourning and the glow of burning vehicles in the North and on the eve of the economic union of Europe, the Irish asked how they should celebrate the Easter insurrection, if at all? Once more I think they do themselves honour in taking up this argument. What other race would question and worry over the political effect of their own mythology so strenuously and for days on end in the feature and letter columns of all their daily papers. Denis Donoghue, for example, Irish scholar of prodigious repute, took on the matter of Yeats and the Easter Rebellion in the *Irish Times*. In old age, said Donoghue, Yeats asked:

> Did that play of mine send out
> Certain men the English shot?

The play he referred to was *Kathleen ni Houlihan*. Kathleen is the incarnation of Ireland, a crone fiercely used by strangers. Only by her children's sacrifices could she be restored to beauty:

> They that have red cheeks
> will have pale cheeks for my sake,
> And for all that, they will
> think they are well paid.

159

Donoghue – son of an RUC constable, as he recounts in his fine memoir *Warrenpoint* – acknowledges that the play probably did help send out certain men the English shot. Nonetheless the heroic act is the heroic act, says Donoghue. 'No heroic image can be refuted. I find nothing silly in the association of Pearse and Cuchulain.'

Certainly, after Easter 1916, posting mere letters would never be the same thereafter, in that Post Office in O'Connell Street where Pearse, McBride, MacDiarmad, MacDonagh, Tom Clarke, Connolly, Ceannt and the others made their resistance.

From within, with all its tall, dimpled-glass windows, the place looks untenable as a fortress. Smaller contingents took possession of other strategic points: the Four Courts, the solider City Hall near Dublin Castle, for example. But I suppose that the way modern revolutionaries begin by seizing the television station, Pearse and the boys needed to seize the centre of the British network of control.

And the common belief is that Pearse wasn't in the market for impregnability anyhow. A poet, he was into metaphors. He would be pleased to know about the old statue of that Ulster god-rogue Cuchulain which stands in the post office: that the Irish brush it with their hands, and in so doing are gesturing towards Irish courage and style.

All the Post Office gods whose faces were gigantically represented on banners in 1966 are now more modestly honoured in a slide show inside the Post Office.

As a foreigner, I found myself with the leisure to step aside from the question of how the Post Office should be remembered. The leisure to ask whether Pearse and the others would have taken up arms without Yeats's play? The leisure to ask whether the IRA would have revived itself in the North if the 1966 celebrations in Dublin had been cancelled. The answer is yes, it would all have happened anyhow. The mythology might not have been quite as rich, but the politics would have been the same.

\*

From O'Connell Street and over the Liffey, it is a short walk south, past Trinity again and the Bank, and up Grafton Street to St Stephen's Green, the town's former grazing common turned into a pleasure gardens by one of the Guinness family. Countess Markiewicz commanded a battalion of rebels here in 1916. All around St Stephen's is Georgian Ireland, the Ireland of Grattan's parliament, when the garrison was well dug in and at some ease, when it saw itself as pre-eminently Irish, when it exhibited the conscience and the grace typified by Dean Swift. Merrion and Fitzwilliam Squares are only a little way east of Trinity and St Stephen's Green, and the varied, bright paintwork on their elegant doors, together with the varied elegant fanlights above, are talismanic Dublin images.

All up Leeson Street, as well as around three sides of St Stephen's Green, the Georgian houses run. In one of them on the south side of the Green the Catholic University, soon to be University College Dublin, began. An early lecturer was deathless Gerard Manley Hopkins, who broke George Moore's rule about the English being no good at their own language.

From St Stephen's Green, as from many other parts of the town, you can see the great spire of St Patrick's, the Dublin cathedral begun in the twelfth century. In the past it must have dominated the landscape. The Catholic pro-cathedral on the north side of the river keeps a lower profile than great St Patrick's, which has a recently restored and unhappily dour exterior but a fascinating inside.

St Patrick's steeple is the only structure which seems exempt from the city's stringent height restrictions. For that is another old-fashioned charm of the place; that only steeples are allowed to scrape the sky. The Dublin corporation has decreed that

Dublin remain on a human scale. You wonder why you feel so comfortable there. Until you remember. There are no hubristic towers. It would be wonderful if the the city corporation could hold out on this question of the height of buildings. It will give the town an increasing novelty for the rest of us. It also might expiate, at least in part, the corporation's crime in having permitted, on the west side of St Stephen's Green, a screamingly out-of-place shopping mall, resembling in part a vast, beached paddle-steamer from a river more gigantic than the Liffey, and a fake-Maharajah's palace which would look phony even in Delhi.

St Patrick's anyhow has, as well as its steeple, a charming interior – it contains the graves of bishops and priests from well before the Reformation, but most people go there for Dean Swift. Although probably not as well read as Yeats and Joyce, his name somehow resonates because of Gulliver and the Lilliputians. Dean Swift's memorial, and the memorial to Esther Johnson, his 'Stella', are instantly signposted in the nave. Even the memorial to his servant Alexander McGeek draws a crowd.

Swift's Latin memorial reads:

> I have gone
> where savage indignation
> cannot torment me.
> Go, pilgrim,
> and strive to imitate
> this strict and devoted
> servant of liberty.

The charm of the epitaph is only partially vitiated by the fact that he wrote it for himself.

All this south side – the Georgian sites, the literary ones, St Patrick's, could be walked around if necessary in a leisurely day. There would still be time for afternoon tea in the Shelbourne or a pint at Doheny and Nesbitt's, an ill-lit but snug venue for journalists and persiflage artists. An intimate place in an intimate city.

All of it a matter of roods and poles and perches, or the very hardest a short bus ride down the coast to Dalkey and Joyce's Martello Tower. ('He looked down on the water and on the mailboat clearing the harbourmouth of Kingstown.')

Or if not Dalkey then out along Dame Street and High Street, past Dublin Castle and so on to the terrible, failed majesty of Kilmainham. There, in an oblong and to-this-day creepy courtyard of high and comfortless stone walls, facing a sky as geometric as a coffin, the 1916 rebels would be cut down by British firing squads. Connolly seated in a chair for his own execution (didn't the British know they were playing into his hands?) because his Post Office wound still debilitated him.

\*

The reason Dublin stimulates us is that we can still feel it, the concentration of the effects; and the afterglow of that extra-ordinary revival, of Joyce's creative love for Nora, of Yeats's for Maude Gonne. As Ulick O'Connor writes in *The Troubles,* we can still feel the after-consecration of Maude's utterance as, hobbling forth in the role of Kathleen ni Houlihan, she elevated Irish history in Yeats's words:

> They shall be remembered forever
> They shall be alive forever
> The people shall hear them forever.

We can feel still therefore the aftershock of the actions and interactions of Joyce and Shaw and Markiewicz and Gonne and Yeats and Gogarty, and of that strange spiritualist George Moore, who said that English on the English tongue was 'a dry shank bone in the dust heap of Empire'. All of them bouncing off each other like super-agitated ions in a pocket handkerchief's space, smaller than a Californian shopping mall. In Nassau and Grafton Streets therefore the air pends with significance, the mana is dense, the names and mysteries spill into each other. The New Worlder who has read anything at all wanders agape in this staid and paltry and exalted space. The young wander here and ask, 'How can we go back and make this all happen in Cleveland or Topeka or Portland or Winnipeg or Adelaide?'

Even the Irish young are intimidated by the mystery. But they have something we don't, a connection to a certain Irish lightning which, correctly sparked, will strike twice in plain old Dublin.

We who learned in antipodean schools amongst gum trees that Ireland *was* the Land of Saints and Scholars also learned that there was a visible sign of this fact. The visible sign was called the *Book of Kells*.

You approach the *Book of Kells* up an alley between two-storey-high book cases. They house a fraction of the library's real books. For Trinity is a library of record, and receives a copy of every book published in England and Ireland. Half a mile of new shelving has to be found each year.

On the way to the library's Number One Book, you pass Brian Boru's harp, though everyone says it is not Brain Boru's; it is fifteenth century. But its lovely gilt evokes a memory of song: 'The Harp that Once through Tara's Halls'.

These are extraordinary products: the *Book of Durrow* and the *Book of Kells*; but they are small for artefacts of such enormous repute. You get the same shock as when you find out how small the *Mona Lisa* is. But what a packed universe on these pages! How can you imagine anything as sophisticated as this coming out of Kells, County Meath, in the late eighth century, early ninth? Or some say it may have come from Iona or Lindisfarne, other monasteries of Columbkille and cul-de-sacs of the modern world. Each page, proliferating with men and women and beasts in extraordinary conjunction, was the work of cunning and patient hours. It drew on the same sort of devices seen in the early Christian chalices, croziers and other ornamentation in the National Museum a few blocks away and up Kildare Street – the Tara Brooch, the Ardagh Chalice, and so on.

The *Book of Durrow* from Columbkille's monastery in Durrow, County Offaly, is even earlier than *Kells*. On each page the same intricate continent, the same richness, the same populace of beasts and prophets, the graphic intricacy of the Latin of the Vulgate Bible. Periodically, the cases in Trinity College Library where the books lie are opened, and a new page turned.

Not to be forgotten in the shadow of *Kells* are other exquisite Trinity College documents: the *Codex Primus Usserianus*, or the *Books of Dimma, Mulling, Armagh*. Or the *Garland of Howth* illuminated by monks on the island called Ireland's Eye, off the mouth of the Liffey. Or the much later *Book of Leinster*. They are like Dublin itself – complicated glory in a small span. They glorify a phase of European history in which sensibility was nearly swallowed up in pettiness and raiding. But not in Kells or Durrow, not in Armagh or Mulling.

While standing looking at a page of *Kells* from the Gospel of St Mark, I heard a museum guard speaking to a friend on the telephone. 'Yes,' he said, 'an exhibition of books on fishing. And there's a competition for anyone who answers a quiz right about fly fishing and trout fishing. I could enter it meself if employees weren't barred out, so I thought your boy might want to enter. He's a paragon, your boy!' A saint. And a scholar.

So the Irish make their arrangements while *Kells* says, in a page of such flamboyance that only a few words can fit on it, *Cum turba multa esset cum Jesu* – When a great crowd was with Jesus.

*

You still encounter beggars in Dublin but for those with jobs, and a sound home, the quality of life in this manageable city is amongst the best in Europe. And it is a city small enough to have retained its traditions of neighbourliness. I remember setting out one morning with a friend who lived south of the Grand Canal. The Royal Canal on the north of the Liffey and the Grand Canal on the south are two great navigational canal works of the Georgian era, and the argument is that to be a true Dubliner you have to live between them. Or at least on the banks, as my friend did.

We were going to buy the *Irish Times*, when we met my friend's next-door neighbour on his doorstep. He invited us in for tea. There is no one more insistent than a Dubliner with an invitation. We found ourselves in a snug kitchen, facing the street, a nest and a vantage point at once. And they were not really drinking tea. The mother of the house was sipping some Cork Dry Gin, a favourite Dublin drink. There is a lot of liquor made in Cork, and the corn whiskey which is blended into Bushmills's standard product comes from Cork. North and South, they say, are at least united in their spirits.

The daughter of the house worked for Guinness. The great Guinness brewery is on the south side of the river, by the Liberties: so called because it once lay beyond the reach of the city's jurisdiction. A great number of Huguenots would settle in the Liberties, and the graves of the Huguenot settlers of the late seventeenth century can be seen in the graveyard on that regular boozers' walk between the Horseshoe Bar at the Shelbourne and the warm, dark snugs of Doheny and Nesbitt's.

Anyhow, the daughter of our hosts who worked at Guinness and had just received her month's quota of the stuff kept offering my friend and I some, and arguing, 'You must go and see the Hop Store in Crane Street.' In forcing us to take a morning Guinness, she used arguments of pure lateral paganism, such as, 'If you don't have one, then you won't know what you've missed out on.' In the end, we drank two big pint glasses. The exquisite creamy head, and the long dark body of the liquid. As Flann O'Brien says, *A pint of plain is your only man*. And as the Dubliners say of that exquisite demarcation between the solid froth and the anthracite nectar: *liquid apartheid*.

By 10.30 in the morning the day had taken on a richer complexion and a potentiality it did not seem to have at 9 a.m. What was most amazing about this hospitality is that it occurred on Good Friday, at the hands of people who meant to attend 'The Stations' (the Stations of the Cross) that afternoon.

Running away south from the Joyce and *Kells* glories, the ordinary suburbs stretch down towards Tallaght. Dalkey and Killiney in the south are Victorian coastal suburbs of great though perhaps not overwhelming charm, though in the Irish tradition Flann O'Brien transmuted the former hilariously in *The Dalkey Archive*. Again, however, the Irish have through their heroic palaver and their advanced capacity to make up stories about themselves turned all the town into more than itself. Bright young Irish people – and a vast part of the town's population is less than thirty years – complain about how restrictive and wrong-headedly quaint it can be, and others say that it is turning into a real European capital under the influence of Ireland's new European connections. They are speaking in part of how that great fortress, Dublin Castle and the State Apartments therein, was tarted up for the meeting of the European Parliament there in 1990; in part of the nightclubs in Leeson Street, the Italian restaurants in Dame Street. They are speaking of the *real, the merely municipal* Dublin.

What counts for the visitor is the Dublin we bring to Dublin in our heads. We put that personal Dublin like a template over the real one and are more or less satisfied. That exercise is what we come here for. Any old city can be *European, cosmopolitan*. And Manchester could as easily be Birmingham, and Leeds could as well be Sheffield. But it is almost trite to say that only Dublin can be Dublin.

People talk about the old Dublin, and how it has died, and yet no other town in Europe has a chance of being Dublin's clone. Still. To hell with Dublin being Paris! Dublin has enough on its plate being the city of our imaginations. That is a task it performs slackly but with ease.

*

While in Dublin, I received a letter from Ionad Oidreachta Duthalla, the Duhallow Heritage Centre. Duhallow is an area of central North Cork lousy with members of my clan, our Gaelic name, O'Connaillaigh or O'Connaillach.

I had gone across to Duhallow from Kenmare, a town beautifully located at the south end of the Ring of Kerry, from the splendour of that great Victorian home now called the Park Hotel whose windows look out on the broad estuary of the Kenmare River and the blue-green Kerry hills. From Kenmare to plain old Newmarket in Duhallow, a village of the Irish heartland, barely remarked upon in the guide books!

Ulick O'Connor, writing of the young Nationalist volunteers who appeared in towns like this to resist British policy in its rather graphic Black and Tan incarnation, says of them, 'The towns and villages they had come from were virtually feudal demesnes.' The memory of this line was with me when I visited my grandfather's village of Newmarket, Duhallow. I had first seen it casually one sunny day in 1976. This time it sat between its hills under the lash of yet another autumn storm. Any old post-feudal town, Republic of Ireland. So far inland, it lacked even the stone towers which marked coastal towns.

It was incorporated by a family called the Aldsworths in the time of James I, and their house stood always on a hill on the southern side of town. The latest version of the Aldsworth home, a very fine Georgian one, with a circular entry hall and a sweeping Georgian staircase, is the quintessential big house which sits on the edge, or if possible, above most villages.

Nearby Mallow on the Blackwater was Newmarket's big town to the south. Mallow had been a place of strong Cromwellian Plantation and became a handsome spa for Anglo-Irish gentry. 'The Rakes of Mallow' gave the place a reputation for profligacy, which, when you look at its light industrial parks and staid streets now, all seems a little unlikely. In the sober late nineteenth century, it billed itself not as a venue for riotous life but as 'the Bath of Ireland'.

The area has other distinctions though: a little to the east of Newmarket, between Buttevant and Doneraile, Edmund Spenser wrote *The Faerie Queene*. Though the poem, despite its merits and frequent grace notes, may sometimes seem flatulent to modern readers, Spenser himself is a fascinating early instance of the English landlord, and of the nature of life, both gracious and besieged, that his class lived in the Irish countryside.

Spenser came to Ireland as a young aide to the Lord Deputy – it was the best that his patron at Elizabeth's Court, Sir Philip Sidney, still a poet but declining in influence, could organise for the young man. In the 1580s Spenser was involved in campaigns against the Fitzgerald-led Munster rebels and their Spanish and Italian supporters. The victory of Lord Gray over the Munster rebels at Smerwick on the Dingle Peninsula was transmuted by Spenser into Artegalle's victory over Grantorto in *The Faerie Queene*.

Spenser held various posts in Dublin, Wexford, Kildare – positions given out as favours and doubly valuable because they could be later sold. Then he came to clerkship of the Council of Munster. The Spaniards were still fighting in Ireland, in the hope of political advantage and out of religious solidarity with the Gaelic lords, and the Gaelic rebels of North Cork were the same Desmond family, the Fitzgeralds, whom the poet had already faced. The Spaniards' willingness to involve themselves would not end until their defeat many years later at Kinsale, that exquisite port at the mouth of the Bandon, and the O'Neills would be defeated with them. That would lead to the Flight of the Earls, the Plantation of Ulster, and ultimately to the most recent violent death in Ulster.

Spenser's reward for his services to Anglo-Munster was the forfeited Desmond castle and estate called Kilcolmán near Doneraile. Its ruins are still there, some eighteen miles east of Newmarket. He came into possession of the property in 1587. One of the sweetest English voices of his day, he was part of the British mechanism of acquisition through Gaelic forfeiture, and he believed in the justice of his handsome three-thousand-acre reward. His possession would not however be trouble-free.

He wrote energetically at Kilcolmán, and a neighbour, Walter Ralegh, persuaded him to travel to London with the first three books of *The Faerie Queene* to invite the patronage of the Queen. What a splendid, gracious, humane planet Spenser occupied! What conversations must have been held in Kilcolmán and Doneraile and Buttevant. What genial love poems he wrote to Elizabeth Boyle, his second wife; Spenser at his finest, his most transparently genuine:

> Tell me, ye merchants' daughters, did ye see
> So fair a creature in your town before,
> So sweet, so lovely, and so milk as she,
> Adorned with beauty's grace, and virtue's store . . .?

The other Ireland, the alternative planet, impinged on his attention only in the form of servants, copious and cheap in a devastated countryside, and then in the form of rebel armies. Otherwise the two versions – the gracious, Puritan, land-endowed world; and the hard, Papist, dispossessed, wattle-and-daub one – rarely touched each other. You can still feel the unreality – two separate worlds packed into the one small area – in many of the residual structures of Anglo-Ireland.

In 1598, the rebellion of O'Neill the Earl of Tyrone reached Cork, and the rebels torched Kilcolmán. Spenser, with other members of the Council of Munster, fled to Cork City. It happened that some two years before the sack and burning of Kilcolmán, Spenser had written his *A Veue of the Present State of Ireland*. He showed some compassion for the ordinary Munster folk. They displayed 'such wretchedness that any stoney heart would have rued the same'. But he recommended a savage policy just the same. He must have been known in the area for mouthing off about what should be done to the natives, since Viscount Roch of Fermoy ordered that 'none of his people should have trade or commerce with Mr Spenser'.

The *Veue* was registered at Stationers' Hall, but had still not been printed at the time of the sack of Kilcolmán – in fact, for largely political reasons, the 'further aucthoritee' Spenser sought for its publication did not emerge until some thirty-four years after his death.

He was made Sheriff of Cork at the urging of the Privy Council, was sent to Whitehall bearing urgent letters from Sir Thomas Norreys, and wrote a report to Elizabeth, 'Out of the ashes of disolacion and wastenes of this your wretched Realme of Ireland.' He died in London during this mission. Both the Anglos and the Irish have pronounced on him. He never appears in Irish anthologies. He is always there in English ones.

*

A later literary glory of the region was Canon Sheehan, parish priest of Doneraile and the author of some lively novels of late-nineteenth-, early-twentieth-century Irish clerical life. *Luke Delmege* and *My New Curate* would have been considered great novels of Duhallow, and certainly they were widely read in religious orders and seminaries throughout the world, receiving the ultimate approval of being theologically sound enough to read from lecterns during dinner time in monasteries from Cork to Calcutta, from Kansas to Western Australia. They were powerful depictions of the central role the priest held in Irish towns: scholar, counsellor, protector, provider of welfare, prime mediator with the occupying power; the Maynooth-educated gentleman-scholar who could speak on equal terms with the gentry.

\*

So much for the district. But Newmarket itself had its remarkable fervours too, and a minor but worthy place on the maps of both Irelands, the Anglo and the native. The Aldsworth mansion on the hill, now the above-mentioned Ionad Oidreacht Duthalla, was the home of Mary Barry, Mrs Aldsworth, who in nearby Doneraile, some time in the 1790s, secreted herself in a clock so that she could spy on a meeting of Freemasons. This spunky adventure had its own strange reward. She was discovered and then admitted to the Order for secrecy's sake. She became renowned amongst the gentry as the first woman Mason.

This was, by the way, a period in which Freemasonry provided a powerful milieu not only for reaction but for revolution. In France, for example, Talleyrand and Lafayette were Masons; in America, Washington and Jefferson. In Ireland, many of the Protestant patriots involved in the Irish uprisings in the late 1790s and early 1800s were also Lodge members.

Newmarket was above all though the hometown of Robert Emmet's beloved, Sarah Curran, daughter of the lawyer and politically moderate Nationalist, John Philpot Curran. With Mrs Aldsworth, Sarah is buried in Newmarket Church of Ireland churchyard. This inspirer of Robert Emmet, and later of the poet Thomas Moore, who wrote a poem celebrating her constancy:

> She is far from the land
> Where her young hero sleeps . . .

Robert Emmet and his brother Thomas were United Irishmen even in their student years, and both of them, after a stint in Fort George prison in Scotland, went to France. Robert Emmet stayed in France for two years, after evading a warrant for his arrest issued by Dublin Castle in 1799. The Emmet brothers – like Tone – wished to add the further influence of French arms to the uneasy connection which already existed between the political thinkers in the United Irishmen, and the inchoate and unfocussed secret armed bands. These bands still existed, a raw and readymade rebel army, holding out after Vinegar Hill, notably in the Wicklow Mountains.

An interview with Napoleon led Robert to dismiss the dithering of other Irish leaders, to return to Ireland and to take impetuous action. He was in Dublin, building up supplies of arms and communicating with the armed bands in the countryside, when an explosion at one of his dumps in Dublin warned the Castle and tipped his hand.

Historians, especially English, and even the witty Robert Kee, are contemptuous of Emmet's uprising. It failed because of certain charming and indisputably Irish flaws in Emmet's character. And agents of the Castle, and messed-up signals between rebels in Dublin, Wicklow and Kildare, ensured that few turned up to support Emmet's drive on Dublin Castle.

With eighty men, who drew in perhaps another eighty on the way to Dublin Castle, Emmet is depicted as retiring in horror when his men met the carriage of Lord Kilwarden, the Lord

Chief Justice of Ireland, and piked him and his nephew to death. So, say the historians, he was disorganised and unrealistic and even – in his only attack on the tyrants – fatuous.

But in terms of what you need to be remembered in Ireland, this young lover of Sarah Curran of Newmarket, Cork, had all the gifts. He advanced on Dublin in the right fashion, wearing a green and white uniform. And like Parnell, he loved his lass. He had moved in from the Wicklow Mountains while on the run so that he could be within reach of Sarah Curran, who was at that stage living near Dublin. With her, he planned to emigrate to America, to a political scene which would have been congenial to his talents. Visiting her a month after the uprising, he was captured near Harold's Cross, and tried and hanged a month after that. He perished stylishly, which is another highly prized Irish talent.

*

But what every man, woman and child in Ireland knows of Emmet is of course his famous speech from the docks: 'Let no man write my epitaph . . . When my country takes her place among the nations of the earth, then and not till then let my epitaph be written.'

Twenty-five years old, he had achieved the correct eloquence to become an Irish god. Seventy-seven years later in Australia, Ned Kelly, the rebel son of an Irish convict, would achieve a similar but more primitive effect with: 'Tell them I died game!'

Thomas Moore, Emmet's classmate at Trinity, wrote two ringing ballads for him, 'Let Erin Remember' and the already mentioned poignant Sarah Curran song, 'Oh Breathe Not the Name', was also composed to honour the love of Emmet and Sarah Curran.

In Newmarket itself she is not vastly respected. In fact my grandfather was raised to disrespect her. For she married promptly enough, and that to a British officer.

But as they say, what's a girl to do? Was she to occupy for a lifetime the niche made for her by Emmet's eloquence and Moore's sanctifying verses? Why shouldn't a woman escape from a compelling ghost like Emmet's and take an ordinary man into her bed?

In any case, Sarah Curran, Newmarket's failed Madonna, is dust now in her graveyard, amongst the disapproving shades of the anonymous Irish.

*

I called them the anonymous Irish – Jeremiah Keneally and Anne MacSwiney – and they were. All their children, born in the Newmarket townland called Glenlara, on the west side of town, vanished to Brooklyn or the antipodes. The standard Irish tragedy. The last one left in 1916 – he would beget eight small Americans by two wives in Brooklyn.

One wonders how it was to know that you would not be followed to your grave in the cemetery named Clonfert, on the west side of Newmarket, by any of your vanished children. In the case of their son Tim, he was by then running a general store called the Harp of Erin beside the Macleay River in New South Wales. The contact with Sydney was by coastal steamer – the railway would not come through until 1917. Their mail made its arduous way there: an 1892 letter from Jeremiah in Newmarket to his son Tim in New South Wales states the Irish griefs, the dependence of home folk on money from the New World, as well as any document I have read:

> We have got Photos, how lovely, how grand. You appear thin but apparently in good health, and all the Connoisseurs of beauty and taste who had the privilege of seeing your Amiable Wife's Photo pronounce her as being far in excellence as could scarcely be seen. On that subject there is a deed of

175

Separation. I Fear an eternal decree that during my life I shall never again see you or Any of my exiled children – which is painful to endure on your part and Ours. In the meantime it is pleasing to hear And know that your brothers and sisters are well. We have lately heard from them one and all with encouraging prospects. May God Continue His Graces to us All. The mere fact of the Photos so joyfully received was near putting out of my mind thanks for the Two Sovereigns last August. And though Much money may be valued, the Photos much exceed as an endearing, everlasting memorial. What would I give if I could only gaze on your lovely Wife and child for one moment . . .

Even the news of Jeremiah's and Anne's deaths had to make its own long passage to Sydney and up the coast by steamer.

All of their children – as I have already mentioned – lie buried a long way from Newmarket, in graveyards from northern and western New South Wales to Brooklyn, Long Island, Connecticut, Boston.

A Newmarket-cum-family myth, sustained in America and Australia and perhaps unreliable, was that Anne MacSwiney was related to the family of 'martyred' Lord Mayor of Cork, Terence MacSwiney. That was one of the claims casually inserted in my brain early in my Australian childhood. If there is truth to it, I for one did not inherit MacSwiney's fine-boned slimness.

More reliable is the question of my grandfather's relationship to John Keneally, a Cork Fenian from the Newmarket townland of Glenlara, whose name has a certain Duhallow eminence.

Without wishing to generate the sort of myth-making which Conor Cruise O'Brien castigates, I have to say that Keneally's career has the averagely astounding complexity and interest you find in the histories of most intelligent transportees. And it gives insights into the way the divisions in Irish society replicated themselves so energetically at the ends of the earth.

The register of transported *Hougoumont* convicts in the archives of Western Australia bears the following notation for him:

> Keneally John, son of James, Glenlara, Cork; unmarried clerk, Glenlara, literate, R.C., CONV. Cork, 14/12/65 [Date of conviction] A buyer to a Cork draper – previously respectable, a centre in F.B. [Fenian Brotherhood] – attended Fenian meetings; treason, felony, 10 yrs penal servitude; Portland Prison (5383); Fremantle Prison, West Guildford Road Party (9795); six letters home, character very good.
>
> Release: Free Pardon 15/5/69; sailed for Sydney on *Rangatira* 21/9/69, then to San Francisco on *Baringa* 21/10/69.

Keneally and a small group of other Fenians in Portland Prison had a significant part in the history of criminology – the first mug shots ever taken were of them. This is a claim which I feel should be honoured in the Newmarket museum in the old Aldsworth house. Placards with numbers were hung round their necks, and they blinked in the phosphorus light. Some of those first mug shots show facial damage. There seem to be some suspicious swellings in Keneally's face, but we can't be sure about it. However, in the case of a soldier Fenian called Thomas Darragh, sergeant in the Second Queens, another Cork man, the signs of the beatings he'd taken are quite visible.

This group's other part in the history of crime was that they were on the very last convict ship to Australia, the *Hougoumont*. By that stage the eastern states of Australia had abolished convictism, but the immense, underpopulated, under-supplied-with-labour colony of Western Australia was still willing to accept ships.

It is significant that I mentioned 'crime' and 'criminology'. In Dublin and Portland and Dartmoor, Keneally and his colleagues had agitated – just as later generations of 'politicals' would – to be recognised as political prisoners. But there were amongst them soldiers, including the great John Boyle O'Reilly, who had rebelled from within the British Army. While Keneally and the others were on board the *Hougoumont*, the civilian Fenians were allowed to keep separate quarters from the general convict population, while the military Fenians – including John Boyle O'Reilly, prize fighter and poet and future novelist – were confined in the hold with the habituals.

The preferential treatment continued when Gladstone decided – as a concession to the Irish – to pardon the *Hougoumont* Fenians. 'My mission is to pacify Ireland,' he announced as rationale.

Through a bureaucratic mix up, only thirty-four of the forty-three civilian Fenians in Western Australia received pardons. The military Fenians, seventeen of them, 'D' for Deserter branded on the chests of a number of them, were not included in the pardons either.

The pardoned civilian Fenians didn't have the resources to leave Western Australia until funds arrived from the Irish community in Victoria and South Australia. Keneally was sent then to the eastern states to investigate the options open to the pardoned men. The Irish diggers on the goldfield in Victoria and New South Wales and New Zealand showed ready sympathy for 'these unfortunate Celts who must beg, borrow or starve ... for all the home officials cared'. A donation of five pounds which came to Keneally from the New South Wales goldfields was signed, 'Vinegar Hill'. There were appeals in Sydney. At last, against the rantings of the Orange Society in the various colonies, an extraordinary sum of five thousand pounds had been collected to enable the pardoned men to leave the penal colony of Western Australia. The money was dubbed the Released Irish State Prisoners' Fund.

The state of Victoria, its parliament in Melbourne, had passed an Influx of Criminals Prevention Act which prevented any transportee whose sentence had not expired three years earlier from spending more than seven days in Victoria. Police met Keneally's ship to inform him of the limit, but with the help of a number of influential Irish Australians, he managed to get permission for a month's stay. He spent the time travelling from Melbourne to the goldfields, met and drank 'good colonial claret' with Charles Gavan Duffy, the Land Leaguer, and was offered a partnership in a dry goods business on the Ballarat goldfields. Unhappily, however, in Sydney earlier that year, an unbalanced Fenian had attempted to shoot Prince Alfred, the Duke of Edinburgh and younger son of Queen Victoria; all this at a Sydney picnic ground named – through the ironies which generally attend such events – Clontarf, after the Dublin seaside suburb.

Gavan Duffy was therefore ultimately unable to persuade the Chief Secretary of Victoria that Keneally and his comrades would make good Australians.

Arrested two days after he had overstayed the deadline, Keneally was found guilty and bound over. The *Advocate*, the Melbourne Catholic paper, spoke of the Chief Secretary's Orange connections, and 'the law's English bigotry'. Keneally's appeal was heard before Chief Justice Redmond Barry, an Ulster man who would later condemn Australia's Irish rebel, Ned Kelly, to hang in Melbourne Gaol.

Keneally, lucky enough to escape further imprisonment, was ordered to leave Victoria. He took off for Western Australia with news that Victoria was not an option. Perhaps New South Wales, where the press had heavily criticised the Victorians, might prove more genial.

At last all the Fenians boarded the *Rangatira* in Albany,

Western Australia, and at each port of call had to assure the police they would not go ashore. In Sydney, the Loyalists were appalled when the Irish community planned a picnic for Clontarf, on the same beautiful bush-girt headland where the Duke had been wounded. The *Sydney Morning Herald* demanded, 'And what have the liberated Fenians done to deserve an ovation where Royal blood was so recently spilt?' But not all the community was so rabid. Keneally writes,

> All the bigotry and anti-Irish hatred of the Orange and Shoneen community were aroused ... and it looked for a while as if there might be some senseless and useless bloodletting. Organisations were getting ready, some drilling going on and old, rusty muskets shined up for service. At this time an old Scotchman, familiarly called 'Jack' Robinson, or Robertson (I forget which) was Chief Secretary of New South Wales. He was considered a fair-minded, good sort of official ... The appointment was made, and Cashman, Hennessy, Fitzgibbon and myself went ... We were introduced to the Chief Secretary, who received us individually in a friendly manner. He explained the object of the meeting and his desire to prevent any unpleasantness in Sydney. He stated the bitter feelings aroused by the announcement of our picnic at Clontarf, and requested our assistance to prevent bloodshed ... Eventually the picnic was abandoned.

Fifteen Fenians chose to embark for San Francisco, including John Keneally. Ten remained in Western Australia, ten returned to Ireland. The Adelaide *Register* wrote, 'Fenianism is not yet extinct in Australia ... thank goodness some of it is going away.'

At the furthest reach of the diaspora, Irish traditions and perceptions and the sense of them-and-us were still being robustly maintained.

*

The prince of all Keneally's fellow Fenians was John Boyle O'Reilly. I know we're a long way from Newmarket in Duhallow for the moment, but some brisk reference to such a consummate Celtic hero is necessary.

It happened that while at Dowth to look at the wonderful Stone Age tombs, I went searching up a country road for the nineteenth-century mansion in which John Boyle O'Reilly was born. I met a pale Englishwoman with a cold, emerging through the mansion's crooked gate and needing a lift down to the local pub so that she could buy Butane to warm the meditation room. For the birthplace of the Fenian is a Buddhist Meditation centre now, bought and paid for by a wealthy American transcendentalist.

I looked through the gate at the tower associated with the hero's childhood, and thought of the passages this darling boy of the Boyne had made: boxer and singer, soldier and Fenian, Western Australian convict and escapee by whaleboat; author and lecturer on the great nineteenth-century circuits in America; newspaper editor. And a final passage, too young, from a perhaps accidental, perhaps deliberate overdose of laudanum.

With the help of an Irish network in Western Australia, O'Reilly would escape aboard an American whaler called the *Gazelle*, go to Boston, become a newspaper editor, a poet, a novelist (*Moondyne* was a novel of transportation to Western Australia) and a regular on the lecture circuit.

Boyle O'Reilly had that Robert Emmet style which is necessary for admission into the Irish pantheon. He wrote from Boston to the prison authorities in Western Australia:

Dear Sir,

I have just seen a copy of the Police Gazette of Western Australia, in which under the head Absconders I have found my name and description. Should you desire any information regarding my affairs I shall be happy to give it to you. Do not perpetuate the stupid folly of printing my name among your criminals. I am far beyond the reach of your petty colony laws; and I really wish to preserve something of a kindly and respectful memory of your country in which I have some dear friends. Should you ever visit the Republic (the US), I shall be happy to see you. As your Gazette is 'published for Police Information only', please tell your officers, especially Sergeant Kelly, once of Bunbury, that I send them my respects.

Yours very truly,

John Boyle O'Reilly

While ever he was at liberty, O'Reilly was plagued by guilt over the military Fenians he had left behind. He was involved with John Devoy, the famous New York Fenian, in the purchase of a New Bedford whaler named *Catalpa*. The *Catalpa* was to make a routine whaling voyage across the Atlantic and Indian Oceans and put into Bunbury, near Fremantle, and rescue the seven Fenians still serving life sentences. Two agents, a New York journalist called John Breslin, and a deputy sheriff of San Francisco named Tom Desmond, under false names and with references from American senators and judges, came to Western Australia. Breslin was greeted as a potential investor. He established contact with the prisoners. Desmond lived a more anonymous life, employed in a carriage works in Perth.

On Easter Monday 1876, all of the military Fenians still

serving sentences, except for one prisoner who was believed to have too close a relationship with the penal superintendent, escaped with Breslin and Desmond aboard the *Catalpa*. They were pursued unsuccessfully by the colonial warship, *Georgette*.

The money to sustain Desmond and Breslin during their long Australian wait for *Catalpa* had been raised by Keneally of Glenlara in Los Angeles.

So exactly did opinion in Australia reproduce opinion in Ireland, so consistently until the 1960s were lines drawn in the same manner in which they are drawn in Ireland, that the rollicking song celebrating the escape was banned on the Australian Broadcasting Corporation's radio network until well into the Vietnam era. Such is the long reach of Ireland's sectarian passions!

> Come all ye screw-warders and jailors,
> Remember Perth Regatta Day.
> Be sure you lock up your Fenians,
> Or the Yankees will steal them away.

\*

Between the Freemason Mrs Aldsworth and the Fenian John Keneally; between on the one hand the honest maids of Duhallow who – in a famous Irish song – pine for the great Muskerry sportsman 'the bold Thaddy Quill', and Sarah Curran on the other, Newmarket is of interest even when battened down beneath an autumn gale, even when its pubs hunker and its churches are cold. A truism to say: there are memories pooled there, between the Aldsworths' hill and the muddy demesne of the dead at Clonfert, which somehow I would sacrifice a great deal to know about. But by accidents of emigration, I have been dealt out. I have another set of secrets. Here, I only scratch surfaces.

# FOURTEEN

The journey was running down. I came over the Wicklow Gap, through high desolations worthy of Donegal, to the lushness of Glendalough, St Kevin's remarkable monastic foundation, and venue for a succession of monastic endeavours and reforms. Its rebuilt great tower was a high haven from Vikings who came raiding up the Vale of Clara from the direction of Rathdrum. I had heard of St Kevin in childhood: a sixth-century kinsman of Tara's Leinster kings. What a paragon of purity he was, a favourite built for the Jansenist streak in Irish Catholicism. At his bed of rock high in the glen he was approached by a woman who lusted for him. He hurled her away from him into the rapids below. What a destiny it is to love or desire one whose life belongs to the Most High God!

We were all meant to behave with Kevin's Anchorite strictness towards women, if ever any came ravening for us.

Through lovely Avoca I came to Parnell's well-made, pleasant, light-filled, and – by the standards of the Garrison – modest house at Avondale. 'Oh have you been to Avondale,' the song asks, 'And wandered in her lovely vale?' Avondale's Great Eagle was something of an absentee, because he served Ireland in Westminster. He caught his death at an open-air Land League meeting in Galway, returned to Kitty O'Shea in England, and died far too young. His body came back to Ireland, to great obsequies. He lies in Glasnevin, Dublin's renowned cemetery. He was a great lover of his fellow Irish, but he knew they had

184

some problems which were endemic and not simply an index of the damage the occupying power had wrought. Yeats wrote a stinging two-liner about this in the last year of his own life:

> Parnell came down the road, he said to a cheering man;
> 'Ireland shall get her freedom and you still break stone.'

\*

I was amused by the terminology of my publisher, who described the big houses I sometimes stayed in as camps. He had tried to set me up with two or three camps in each of the kingdoms: Ulster, Leinster, Munster, Connaught. One of my Leinster camps was Tinakilly House in Wicklow. It owed its spaciousness, its great hallway and its vistas of the Irish Sea to the rewards heaped on its owner, Captain Robert Halpin, Confederate blockade runner, then captain of Brunel's giant steamship, the famous *Great Eastern*.

He commanded the immense *Great Eastern* during its years as a cable layer, a career which altered the condition of humankind and made the instantaneous transmission of messages a fact of the world. Intelligence which had been dependent on the speed of horses and even human runners was now liberated by a Wicklow man from its merely muscular limitations. Halpin laid ocean-bottom cable from Kerry to the Canadian coast, from Brest to Newfoundland, from Madeira to South America. After permitting deep to speak to deep in this way, he built great Tinakilly, filled it with wonderful maritime paintings, and then fulfilled the latencies of what he'd wrought by dying of a minute injury; blood poisoning from a wound in his toe.

Another Leinster camp of mine was in Maynooth in the north of Kildare. My home there was a plush house called Moyglare Manor, a property which had been granted to a Bartholomew Arabin, a Huguenot aide to King Billy's general the Duc de Schombert at the battle of the Boyne. The manor itself is enormous and plushly fitted out in an unabashed, full-throated Victorian manner.

Is it merely my rustic origins, or is it the case that many great Williamite families fared poorly over the long haul? The Arabin family lost grand Moyglare in the 1940s, after many Arabins had died in battle. The mother of the last owner had been struck with lightning while he was in the womb. Maynooth people darkly say the balance of his mind was thus fatally disturbed from the start, and that was the reason he lost Moyglare.

Maynooth is the site of the great seminary which has been mentioned elsewhere in this account of a journey. It was established by an act of the Irish Parliament in 1795, an authorised establishment in a time of official British persecution. It set the tone by which the clergy in Ireland and the New World operated, and so it has a lot to answer for and a lot to be proud of. It sent ten thousand elite priests into the world at large. But when I tried to go to vespers there on a Sunday evening, I found its great chapel locked up. For Maynooth is now a secular and co-ed university. It has even spread beyond the bounds of the neo-gothic seminary, vast in its own right, to extend in cream brick northwards on the far side of the N4. The laughter of women students can be heard in this place once sacred to the robust but frequently tormented celibate clerics. There seem to be few seminarians amongst the ordinary students. Perhaps we are not seeing the last flicker of the powerful Irish clergy. The evidence of Maynooth, however, does not hold out great promise for the future of the clergy as Ireland has known it.

Maynooth was, not to be too irreverent, the great stud of Catholicism. The same limestone from which the seminarians were nourished with living water produced the supreme animals of the Irish: thoroughbred horses. The Irish National Stud is south of Maynooth, at Tully. It had been owned by the British government until the 1940s, when the British handed it to the government of the Republic. It stands of course near the Curragh, the broad majestic limestone plain from which the great grandstands of the Curragh course arise. Ireland has more race courses than any nation its size, even though the famed Phoenix Park Track was closed for good during my stay in Ireland.

In Leinster you run continually up against advertisements for studs and the horses they produce. 'Important winners bred or sold by Airlie Stud in recent years include: Paddy's Sister, Martial, Skymaster, Dark Issue, Glad Rags, Falcom, Pitcairn, Mark Anthony . . .' This country is also one of the last strongholds of fox hunting, much mocked by George Bernard Shaw but still starting on time every October and ending in March. 'All over the country there are recognised packs, making it possible to hunt seven days a week during the season,' the literature boasts.

There must be few places on earth left that can make such an offer without fear of the moral outrage of animal liberationists. The sport of the Long Occupation remains, even though the seminary of the Long Occupation seems to have utterly changed its nature.

*

There is a final question any writer returning from a visit to Ireland is always asked: are the Irish good writers because they're good talkers?

What you notice is that they are talkers in a lateral as well as vertical plane. I stopped for a pint towards dusk in Corofin, a beautiful little town on the edge of the Burren, that stretch of stony country in Clare scattered about with neolithic graves and dolmens. As well as myself, there were two farmers in the bar of a little pub called McNamara's. I ordered half a pint of Guinness from Mrs McNamara. She said, 'Do you mind, sir, if I just finish pouring two pints for these fellers here? Because as the man says, I've never seen a living man standing round dead of hunger, but I've seen plenty of 'em standing around dead of thirst.' That *man* is frequently invoked in Ireland, and he has a Wittgensteinian competence with the language and limits of meaning.

A citizen I gave a lift to one grim morning north of Leenaun, Galway, asked me characteristically when we arrived at the little village where he wanted to make a phonecall whether I had time for a pint. The Anglo-Saxon writ which fiddles around with formulas about sun and yard-arms doesn't run in Galway. Of course, what he was really asking for was an exchange of more than information: stories.

He asked me was I married, and in return I asked him the same question. He said no, but that it had nearly happened to him once. His job as a buyer for woollen mills took him to a lot of towns in Connemara, and he said that he had never had any trouble falling in love. But no sooner would it happen than that he would move on. Contact would be lost.

And so in southern Connemara he met a girl for whom he *really* fell. He went out with her twice, and then she told him that she was planning to emigrate to the United States. She had her fare paid and everything ready. He said that he understood, but he wondered could they meet again, at the interval at the dance in the town of Casla on the following Friday night.

But around Thursday a terrible gale came in from the Atlantic (he was telling me this while a gale was actually blowing) and water rose above the low points of the roads of Connemara. He made an attempt to get to Casla, imagining her waiting in the hall, but he gave up when the enterprise became suicidal. The water was over the roads for nine days, and by the time it went down she had left Ireland.

Half a dozen years later she returned to the area, to the very pub in which we were enjoying a mid-morning pint. She had an American husband. She greeted the wool buyer warmly, kissing him, but when her husband went to the toilet to void off the pressure of generously bought pints, she kissed your man more frankly, with a generous mouth, and told him that he had always been her great love.

He answered that he had tried to get to Casla that night but that the floods had stopped him; that he could imagine her sitting wanly on a bench, wondering what the hell, and then going home again and taking off for America. She said, 'Oh, but I couldn't get there either. We were totally flooded out too.'

What I liked about this story was the way it required his grief to change gear after its many a year in the same mode.

Like the Leenaun storyteller's tale, some of the stories about themselves which people told me in Connemara were so artistically complete I suspected that given the leisure to write the stuff down they would all be James Joyce or at least Sean O'Faolain. It didn't matter if they were absolutely accurate stories at all – in fact they had more artistic merit if they weren't. But it is sometimes as is if novels fall readymade from the generally ambiguous Irish sky.

It took a well-known Irish writer and University College Dublin professor about thirty minutes to tell me a tale about how when he was a boy he went doing good works around the drying-out sanatorium which was located in a Cistercian monastery near Dublin. 'Going to the Cistercians' has an equivalent meaning in Ireland as 'going to the Betty Ford' has in the United States. At the Cistercians this professor knew there was a particularly muscular monk called Brother Albrecht, champion aversion therapist, a man designed by temperament and vocation to bring the detoxifying Irishman to his senses. The professor recounted how one day, outside a window of the monastery, he heard the following conversation between Brother Albrecht and a tenuously recovering alcoholic. 'Now, sir. Be a good fella and come out from under the bed.'

NOW AND IN TIME TO BE

'Fuck off outta that! Yeh brown bastard!' (In those days, Cistercian lay brothers wore brown.)

Again, in this cybernetic age the Irish have an ambition still to find time for what they call crack (song, laughter, stories, all to the accompaniment of liquor). I have already mentioned their cynicism about being too clever and too efficient. I wonder if the technocrats and whiz kids of the EC will ever change the Irish, ever try to make them as sharp and focussed as the Japanese. It will be a battle, for the Irish treasure their indolent air with a nationalist fervour. With a theological zeal too. Eight hundred years of punishment has bred in them an inevitable suspicion of the limits of smartness, of information rendered in bytes, and of brisk schedules. An Irish journalist said one day, 'Jesus, Mary and Joseph, I feel like an American today. I've had a breakfast meeting and been to the dentist and it's still only eleven o'clock.' She looked on breakfast meetings as tempting the gods of worldly fatuity, the ultimate deities of Ireland, the mocking destinies with whom we began this journey, the ones who can only be held off by your beating them to the punch, by your showing that you take yourself with the same flippancy they do.

For this very reason – the whimsical deities who inhabit Ireland – myth still holds out well there. I met an academic called Dáithí Ó hÓgaín who has just produced a big dictionary of Irish legend and folklore. I was astounded to find that he is able to list mythological and folkloric stories about the nineteenth-century politician, Daniel O'Connell. I asked Dáithí about Michael Dwyer, a Wicklow rebel who was transported to Australia after the rebellion of 1798 and who lies in an ornate but subsiding mausoleum in Waverley cemetery in Sydney. And sure enough, in Wicklow there are still extant myths about Dwyer. For example, they say one day British soldiers were looking for him, and he hid behind a ferocious sow in a sty. As the soldiers approached the sow O'Dwyer agitated its hind legs and made it grunt fiercely at the soldiers. The soldiers thereby believed that no mortal could occupy the same sty as the sow.

This is a tale worthy of the cycle of stories about Finn McCool, the giant who built the famous causeway in the beautiful but tormented Ulster county of Antrim.

You do get the sense that reckless mythologising may have only now begun to cease being the major sport and spiritual enrichment of the Irish, who could always raise their tales higher than the taller regiments of the enemy.

On my last dusk in Ireland, I left good company and went out into the Dublin rain to find my way over the Liffey and through the northern suburbs of Dublin to the airport. I was so sad I was going to mere London, the capital of a different spiritual empire. The boot which would not close, the one which had so troubled the security forces of Northern Ireland, had something which I could not manage to carry away with me, a folder full of heavily read Bord Fáilte brochures on various counties. Tim Magennis had given them to me. I looked at the folder, in the scant light and slanting rain, and decided to leave them there, to be taken by someone. After all, I had had the best of Ireland, and they might be of use to a later traveller who inherited the vehicle when it had a mended boot. Or else they might be of use to the mender of the boot.

For Ireland is so immense in significance that even the natives require guides and information.

The Publishers gratefully acknowledge the assistance of the following:

Bord Fáilte, Irish Tourist Board, Dublin (telephone: 765871). Hilary Finlay, Irish Country Houses and Restaurants Association, Navan (046-23416). Ivan & Myrtle Allen, Ballymaloe House, Cork (021-652531). Francis Brennan, Park Hotel Kenmare, Kerry (064-41200). Peter & Moira Haden, Gregan Castle, Clare (065-77005). Anne & Patrick Foyle, Rosleague Manor, Galway (095-41101). Dermot & Kay McEvilly, Cashel House, Galway (095-31001). Constance Aldridge, Mount Falcon Castle, Mayo (096-21172). Bob & Robin Wheeler, Rathmullan House, Donegal (074-58188). Terence McEniff, Mount Errigal Hotel, Donegal (074-22700). Joseph & Margaret Erwin, Blackheath House, Londonderry (0265-868433). Graeme & Joan Hall, Glassdrumman Lodge, Down (03967-68451). Norah Devlin, Moyglare Manor, Kildare (286351). William & Bee Power, Tinakilly House, Wicklow (0404-69274). Edward Kearns, Waterford Castle, Waterford (051-78203).

Special thanks are due to Joseph O'Connor, Judy Chrimes and Gary Day-Ellison.

# INDEX